"A beautiful story of faith and doubt, bravery and fear, safety and risk. Lauren's vulnerable writing is a balm to an anxious soul. Different, yet familiar. A reminder that the world is bigger than our own bubble and we are capable of more than we think."

—April Ajoy, author of *Star-Spangled Jesus*

"*Eat Pray Love* meets Amy Peterson's deconstructed missionary memoir, *Dangerous Territory*, in this travelogue of grief, faith deconstruction, complex trauma, and, ultimately, healing. Full of wisdom and compassion for those like her who have faced their own versions of 'breaking,' Cibene is a gentle guide for those of us whose faith has shifted or broken. But more than anything else, I recommend this book because it's a good story. I couldn't stop reading this book, and I dare you to try."

—Liz Charlotte Grant, author of *Knock at the Sky*

"Lauren Cibene's journal of self-discovery and growth may seem highly specific—battling anxiety and low confidence while traveling across India for several overseas projects. But her journey is universal. In today's black-and-white world, the path of wisdom gets shrouded in a fog of gray. Lauren's story serves as a guideline through the fog."

—Sarah Henn Hayward, author of *Giving Up God*

"When our trust in God, humanity, and ourselves is shaken to its core by trauma and betrayal, how do we re-gather the pieces of who we are and rebuild stronger than ever before? *Tiger in a Lifeboat* is a beautifully written memoir of this kind of healing. Grab tightly to the tail of the tigress within you and join Lauren Cibene for a courageous, candid, liberating journey."

—Liz Cooledge Jenkins, author of *Nice Churchy Patriarchy*

"There are books you read, and then there are books you experience—this is one of the latter. Lauren has created a tapestry of pain and transformation that feels deeply personal and profoundly universal. If you've ever found yourself standing in the ruins of what you once believed, *Tiger in a Lifeboat* will remind you that faith can be rebuilt and joy can be recultivated . . . one trembling step at a time."

—Kristen LaValley, author of *Even if He Doesn't*

"We have all needed Lauren's voice and didn't know it until now. *Tiger in a Lifeboat* threads the needle of being willing to walk away after disillusionment from faith and fighting for bright and beautiful hope. It is real, relatable, and an important story for anyone who has ever wrestled with God."

—Raj Lulla, author of *The Caring House*

"Stories worth reading are written by those courageous enough to tell the truth. They make us uncomfortable yet wonderfully seen, affirming where we are while pushing us forward as spiritual companions. *Tiger in a Lifeboat* is such a story—raw, honest, and beautifully told. Along the way, I got to know Lauren and experienced India through her eyes—its people, culture, and life-giving spirit, which shaped both her journey and mine."

—Matt Reynolds, founder of Stoke and Medici House/Medici Nights

"*Tiger in a Lifeboat* is a carefully told tale, not a tell-all, but a tell-just-this. Cibene invites her reader into the universal story of pain and suffering, with a south Asia twist. Cleverly weaving her own story with the classic *Life of Pi*, she gives heft and frame to the million little ways we heal our pain."

—Lore Ferguson Wilbert, author of *The Understory*

Tiger in a Lifeboat

Tiger in a Lifeboat

DISCOVERING INDIA, DECONSTRUCTING FAITH, AND DECIDING TO TRUST AGAIN

LAUREN CIBENE

lakedrivebooks.com

Lake Drive Books
6757 Cascade Road SE, 162
Grand Rapids, MI 49546

info@lakedrivebooks.com
lakedrivebooks.com
@lakedrivebooks

Publishing books that help you heal, grow, and discover.

Paperback ISBN: 978-1-957687-65-0
E-book ISBN: 978-1-957687-66-7

Library of Congress Control Number: 2024926839

Cover design by Fruitful Design, LLC
Author photo by Joseph Baum

Dedicated to the tiger pacing its cage within you.

And to Juju.

Contents

1
The Breaking

Heartbreak hurts the worst in the mornings.

There's a moment between sleeping and waking when you don't remember the thing that shattered you. It's just another normal morning, and then you remember. You remember the pain, the questions, the crack down the middle. In an instant it all comes rushing over you, and you relive it before your feet even hit the floor.

You soon realize you'll never wake up to a "normal" morning again. Your life is bisected now into the days before that great Breaking—and the days after it.

For me, at least, heartbreak hurts worse in the mornings. Even now, as I count every one of the days after my own Breaking, there are still some mornings I wake up, and my stomach lurches into that familiar drop, my chest tightening as if trying to hold my heart in place. Not every morning. But some.

It didn't happen this morning, but as I wake from fitful sleep in my airplane seat, my chest tightens for another reason as the captain and crew prepare us to land in Kathmandu, Nepal. The man sitting across the aisle from me sketches the sign of the cross over himself again and again and again. He's doing it for the same reason my stomach can't seem to stay in place. We're anxious because what we're about to do is risky.

Of the approximately forty-four thousand airports around the world, Nepal is home to several of the most dangerous. Just a month ago forty-nine people were killed when a plane approached a runway at this same airport from the wrong direction, crashed, and burst into flames.

In my dingy plane seat, I am like a kid in a quiet house after watching a scary movie. I overhype every little sound and vibration the plane makes on its descent. The tiny arteries inside my left ear expand as my blood pressure spikes and muffles my hearing. My fingers worry my cuticles until blood blooms in the grooves of my nails.

But miraculously, with a shudder and a groan, the plane stops. We get our things. We wait our turn. And, with a certainty that I have just cheated death, I step into the Nepali sunshine.

This is a bigger deal than you might think. About three months prior (and a little over a year after my own great Breaking), I was borderline agoraphobic. I dreaded leaving my house. My body physically resisted by manifesting debilitating cramps, headaches, and trembling. The days when I got out of bed and showered like a "normal person" were huge victories.

I wasn't always like this. I was made into this person in the aftermath of my Breaking.

Because you are already wondering, I'm not going to tell you about the specifics of my own Breaking. Specificity can get in the way sometimes. It makes for a good therapy session but a poor conversation. And I want this to be a conversation.

I don't want you to feel like you are just a spectator to my tragedy. I'm betting that you have walked through enough tragedy in your own life already:

The loss of something that should've been—would've been—yours.

The crumbling of relationships that were meant to be dependable.

The abuse of power by people we thought we could trust.

A disease that, if it'd just been caught sooner, might not have been so dire.

Miscarriage and chronic illness and abandonment and assault and the finality of death—this might only be scratching the surface.

We've both seen some tragedy. And I'm hoping that, rather than spectating, you feel like we're walking through this journey side by side. When I talk about my trauma, imagine it's the same as yours. Whatever it is that broke your heart, feel free to paint that on me. Let me help you carry it, at least while you're here in these pages.

I will tell you this one detail, because I speak about it explicitly, and your story might not share this theme: my Breaking was caused by the decisions and actions of someone else. Someone I trusted. Someone who was supposed to be a safe place. But they made a choice that left me shattered.

That's how a lot of our Breakings happen, isn't it? Someone decides something. Maybe it's thoughtless: they were distracted, they were stressed, they were inebriated, they were tired.

Or maybe it's deliberate: they had a plan, they had a reason, they had a hunger, they weren't sorry.

But either way, someone makes a decision, which leads to an action, which leads to a Breaking. The notes are different, the song is the same. And people like you and me are left to pick up the pieces.

I never saw mine coming.

What resulted, for me, was a complete obliteration of trust, not just in the one person who instigated my Breaking, but in everyone and everything. If this person whom I trusted so freely was unsafe, then no one was truly trustworthy. Not people. Not God, not the universe. Not myself. Especially not myself.

I felt like I was the one who was ultimately to blame because I was the one who bet it all on black and then lost so spectacularly. *Should I have seen this coming? Could I have prevented it?* My brain performed acrobatic "if-then" maneuvers, and in every single one, I found a way to prove myself guilty.

This was nonsense, of course. This was a desperate brain looking for something it could both blame and control. The belief it latched onto was that if I had some control over the guilty party, I could prevent this from ever happening again. But it would be years before I understood the fallacy here.

Until then, I believed I was untrustworthy and complicit in my own Breaking. After a while this morphed from emotional perception to accepted fact. It was just how it was, and I was certain there was nothing that could repair it.

That's all I'll say about my own specific Breaking, because this book is not about that.

It's about everything that happens after.

When you experience a traumatic event, a thing you never thought could happen, not even in your darkest nightmares, the likelihood of every other tragic event seems to exponentially skyrocket. Plane crashes. Car crashes. Being stabbed or shot or beaten. Anything is possible because the impossible has already happened.

So when I say that my days were filled with dread, it's hard to pin down what it was exactly that I dreaded. Almost everything felt thin and friable, so I was afraid of almost everything:

Of being hurt.
Of being misunderstood.
Of being betrayed.
Of being noticed.
Of both being known and unknown.
Of my loved ones dying, or dying myself.

It was debilitating.

This wasn't supposed to happen. I was a dyed-in-the-wool evangelical who had done everything right for the entirety of my life. My parents educated me at home. They were and are loving and nurturing and intentionally raised their four children so that we wouldn't be exposed to fill-in-the-blank.

We went to church every Sunday and every Wednesday night. I knew all the books of the Bible and could recite swaths of scripture. I'd write them on my bathroom mirror in dry-erase marker and tape them to the interior of my hand-me-down Ford F-150 pickup truck.

I spent every summer in vacation Bible school and then, later, apologetics camps where we learned how to debate and disprove other world-views (I ate that shit up).

I graduated with a film degree, determined to tell stories that "advanced the Kingdom," from a Christian university founded by a prominent televangelist.

I married the blond-haired, blue-eyed son of missionaries. When I kissed him at the altar, he was the only man I'd ever kissed because I was serious about those extreme purity oaths I'd made when I was a brace-faced ugly duckling with banana bangs.

My life had been structured to create a titan of faith, but the Breaking turned this life, along with so much of what I thought about myself and my fellow humans, to ash in my hands. And the God I knew so unequivocally in my girlhood, the one I would normally turn to in moments of crisis, dissolved into the inky black aftermath. His promises of a grand divine plan—a meaning, a purpose, a heavenly repose at the end of all things—vanished along with him.

It's hard to explain what this feels like to someone who has never experienced it, this loss of faith. The loneliness and despair and self-loathing. The lucky ones will never understand.

The lucky ones will say something like, "If your faith crumbles during a hard season, maybe you never had faith to begin with."

Or, "If you feel like God is far away, then you're the one who moved."

The lucky ones will never understand.

After my Breaking, I spent countless days filled simultaneously with surging panic and crippling helplessness. For countless nights I was plagued with intense nightmares and obsessive nihilistic thoughts.

I was left staring slack-jawed at my life and my identity. How could I even begin to rebuild, reestablish, reclaim all that had evaporated?

Anxiety said, "What if you never get back what you lost?"

Depression said, "What does it matter anyway?"

Something was profoundly wrong. I needed help. I wasn't just experiencing an isolated Breaking; I was continuing to shatter day after day after day.

Like a frog slowly boiling to death, I didn't realize how deeply in crisis I was. But in the moments when I caught a glimpse of how desperately I needed help, I explained away my symptoms or minimized my suffering: *Why can't you just move on? Other people have experienced far worse than you. Get over it.*

It wasn't until six months had passed that I finally came to grips with my condition, got help, and began the process of healing. I was diagnosed with post-traumatic stress disorder (PTSD) and PTSD-related anxiety and depression. I had my work cut out for me.

In Yann Martel's novel *Life of Pi*, a young Indian man has his own Breaking. In his case, though, it is not caused by the choices of someone else; it is a freak, random, senseless, horrific event. The terrible un-luck of the draw.

After the ship carrying his family and their entire zoo goes down, Pi is stranded at sea in a lifeboat with a Bengal tiger named Richard Parker. Facing the death of his family and the loss of his entire world, his future, and potentially his life, Pi is forced to adapt or die. He survives, and by the end of the book, you realize that maybe there was no tiger after all.

Pi's mind bisected itself and fabricated a tiger because it was what he needed to survive. Pi was the tiger, and the tiger was Pi.

Pi was timid. The tiger was fierce.

Pi was weak. The tiger was strong.

Pi was afraid. The tiger was courageous.

Sometimes their roles would flip: the tiger would be hungry, and Pi would care for him. But together they were always two sides of the same person. Coexisting, equally true.

As I drifted in my own metaphorical lifeboat after my Breaking, I willed myself to find some inner alter-ego like Richard Parker. Fracking deep into my soul for anything resembling tiger stripes, I struggled to pull myself out of fear and despair and into courage and ferocity. For a while I wasn't even sure this was possible outside of fiction.

Finally, after working with my therapist, I realized that maybe I would need to start acting like a tigress before I felt like she had completely arrived. That was terrifying.

When I felt scared, instead of staying at home, I would need to be brave.

When I felt vulnerable, instead of coiling in on myself, I would need to stay open.

When I felt despair, instead of giving into it, I would need to look for the light.

It was at this point, over a year into my struggle, that my husband Tim said, "Wouldn't it be crazy if we went to India? We've always wanted to go, and flights to Delhi are super cheap right now. This amazing tour is also on sale. But we would have to go soon, like in the next two months. What do you think?"

Before I could even wrap my head around the idea, I heard a tigress growl, "Let's do it."

In an out-of-body experience, I watched our tickets get purchased, our time-off requests get approved, and our bags get packed. My therapist encouraged me and affirmed that I was ready, that I had done the work to support my healing through this kind of decision. That I could do this.

My suddenly emergent tigress ran headlong into a whole new, foreign world that would aggressively rub up against some of my most tender wounds. I just clung to her tail. With a very real fear and a thousand reasons to change my mind, I was about to trust fall into the arms of humanity.

———

The tour company calls our route The Pilgrimage, and it starts in Kathmandu, Nepal's capital city. The plan is to road trip to a few other Nepali cities before crossing the border into India. We'll then hit a bunch of Indian cities I can barely pronounce, much less find on a map, before ending up in Delhi. I know we'll be visiting the Taj Mahal. I know we'll experience sprawling street markets and famously mischievous monkeys and the Ganges River. But I don't know the other people we'll be joining on the tour bus.

I've traveled with strangers before. Before the Breaking. Before I turned into this collapsed mess of a human. Now the idea of being around people all day for the duration of this trip sets my teeth on edge and ties my stomach in knots, but I push it to the back of my mind as we trek across the cracked Kathmandu runway.

We enter a cement building right off the runway. It reminds me of my dilapidated post office back home. Only about half of the fluorescent lights in the ceiling are turned on, making the space feel closed down. Like we stumbled in after hours.

Around me, my fellow travelers are as diverse as the world itself—Planet Earth in microcosm. I hear French, Mandarin, Australian, and British accents, and in front of me a young woman holding a blue and gold Ukrainian passport is struggling to stay awake. Some people are clearly climbers with the Everest Base Camp in their sights. Others are obviously religious pilgrims in the birth country of the Buddha.

We join the long queue to get our visas. Every resource online said that travelers destined for Nepal should plan to do this at the airport after arriving. This instruction gave me persistent heartburn.

What if they refuse to let us in?
What if some quota is instated the day before we arrive, and they turn us away?
What if we need some legal document and can't access it once we're there?

As we inch our way closer to the visa application machines, we can see people getting frustrated. Anxiety's ears perk up, and it cranks up the volume on all these worries in my head. *I tried to warn you.*

Turns out the visa machines have no attendants. The user interface is confusing, and the few instructions that exist are only available in English. I'm relieved that we'll be able to read the prompts at least, but the tightness in my chest only incrementally loosens.

The Ukrainian woman in front of me suddenly turns around and faces me, her eyes puffy with fatigue. Her hair is wrapped in a scarf. A long, straight skirt falls just above the laces of her hiking boots. She holds out her passport to me.

I hesitate a minute, unsure of what's happening. But then I notice that, at the other machines, English speakers have stepped up. Using rudimentary sign language, they point to fields on the screen and then to the lines in their fellow travelers' passports indicating what information is needed to fill out their application.

She's asking me to help her because I can read the English prompts.

Standing shoulder to shoulder, I help her type in her passport number, her name, her date of birth—hypersensitive information that I would never have shared with anyone, much less a stranger from another country. We get her visa application filled out and submitted success-fully. I hand her passport back, but she doesn't walk away. She stands right beside the machine, swaying a little and rubbing her tired eyes as Tim and I fill out our own applications. Once we finish, we head toward the next stage of the process. She falls in step beside me.

She sticks with us through all the different stages of entering the country: visa application, currency exchange, receiving our visas and, finally, admission into the country. We stand in lines together for hours, unable to speak many words between us. But we smile at each other.

Remember, now, that one of the clever little lies Anxiety has been whispering in my ear since the Breaking is that humans should not be trusted. Especially the ones who are different from me. *They are wicked and treacherous and selfish and conniving. They destroy the earth and each other and everything good.*

The reason this lie is clever is because once it is planted, it is like the hardiest grass: almost anything will make it grow. Anxiety says, "Humans are not to be trusted." And Depression says, "It's true, just listen to the news." Depression waters the seeds that Anxiety plants, and the resulting weeds have tripped me up and choked me out of so many beautiful experiences. They've kept me from seizing opportunities to learn. To try my hand at something new. To make friends. To dance.

These experiences are our birthright as humans, some of the best parts of being alive, and I've turned so many of them down. Because I was untrusting and afraid.

I don't wish to minimize the fact that humans are capable of great evil. We are. But to focus on our capacity for evil without giving equal airtime to our capacity for good is unbalanced at best and delusional at worst. There's another subtle trick in Anxiety's lie: It's never, "*We* are untrustworthy." It is always, "*They* are untrustworthy." Such a deadly sleight of hand that fuels racism, sexism, ageism—almost all the *-isms*.

It's easy to know this. It's easy for my brain to recognize this and for my mouth to verbalize it in therapy sessions. "Not all people are treacherous. Not all people have an ulterior motive . . ." But to believe in the inherent good of people enough to drag yourself to the other side of the world and put yourself at their mercy? This is much, much harder.

And yet, I just witnessed it happen.

In this shabby little airport, watching total strangers help each other navigate clunky visa machines, I feel a flicker of sunshine on my soul. Yes, humans may maliciously steal each other's identities. But they also help each other apply for visas in Nepalese airports.

We jump into a taxi after exiting the airport, finally waving goodbye to our Ukrainian friend. Other motorists buzz around us, observing no apparent lanes or signs or speed limits—or vehicle capacity limits. This is my first encounter with South Asian traffic, and it will never pale in its ability to flood my senses.

We zoom through alleyways that look too narrow for our car by several inches, yet somehow we make it out to the other side without losing our side mirrors. It is hot inside the car, but when the windows are rolled down, the dust from the road makes it impossible to breathe.

Crisscrossing above all the dust and honking vehicles are hundreds of high-line wires. They wrap around the tops of telephone poles like spaghetti noodles in the prongs of a fork before dispersing in every direction. My subconscious scribbles down careful notes like some sort of self-appointed safety inspector.

Tim keeps cheesing at me, saying incredulously, "We're in Nepal right now! Can you believe we're in Nepal right now?!" He lives for this kind of stuff. A little over six feet tall, Tim is broad and strong. He's towered over everyone we've seen here. He tans easily, but his eyes and his hair are light—another thing that makes him stick out in this part of the world. Even so, he's calm and at ease in his new surroundings. Born in Israel to missionary parents who moved their family to Scotland halfway through his childhood, Tim is not intimidated by international travel. Honestly, he thrives on it. He has an easy way about him that allows him to make friends anywhere with anyone, even across cultural and linguistic barriers.

He is my opposite. I'm short, pale with dark features, and introverted. He's the golden retriever to my black cat. He anticipates a glass half full while I run through worst-case scenarios. He is courageous; I am cautious. He is the sail to my anchor.

We arrive at the hotel and drop our bags in our room before meeting up with the tour group in the small, humid hotel restaurant. The big window facing the street is streaked with condensation. The handful of wobbly tables and chairs have been pulled together so our eight-person group can sit in a circle. Our tour mates are all women with the exception of our male guide, Adnan, who looks to be in his mid-forties.

Everyone introduces themselves, giving their name and where they're from: four from Australia and two from Canada, making Tim and I the only Americans. Even with travel weariness, all six of the women seem ready, confident, and well-equipped. They're all fit. They're all well-traveled, seasoned pros when it comes to adventures like the one we're now on together. I feel dumpy and untested next to them.

"So, how old is everyone?" Tim asks the group.

"Wouldn't you like to know?" One of the blonde Australians smirks, making eyes at him. I stay quiet. Thankfully, another person answers, and then another, and then another, and the conversation moves on. Everyone is in their mid-twenties, the same age as Tim and me. This isn't surprising; the tour company has age caps on their offerings, and only people under thirty are eligible for this trip.

Adnan gives us a rundown of how our time together will go, outlining safety concerns and logistics. Now that I am finally sitting still, exhaustion begins to set in, and my mind becomes thick and muddled. My arms feel heavy, and my shoulders sag. If I were to lie down right now, I would easily sleep for hours. But as Adnan wraps up the housekeeping, the group decides to go out into the city to get dinner together, and I can see that my extroverted husband really wants to go too.

Right on cue, the tigress saunters in. "Yeah, let's go get some dinner." Once I'm on my feet again, I'm glad we do. Kathmandu is electric with excitement.

"It's the Hindu New Year's Eve," Adnan shouts as we join the noisy throng that fills the dirt streets. His voice competes with the sounds of traffic and music blaring from shops. Hundreds of colorful *lungta* prayer flags stretch from building to building along with strings of lights. Doorsteps and windowsills glow with oil lamps shaped just like the one you might remember from Disney's *Aladdin*. I learn the Hindu calendar is different from the Gregorian calendar. It combines lunar and solar cycles to determine the date, and the new year starts in the spring. This celebration is for the last few hours of the Hindu year 2074.

We wind our way around piles of rubble and parked cars. The city is so tight. The buildings, the roads—everything is so close together. I anxiously remember the earthquakes and mudslides that slammed

Nepal in 2015, just a few years prior to our trip. The thought of such an event hitting this city with its buildings like so many side-by-side Jenga towers makes my stomach drop. I push the thought to the back of my mind as our group ventures up a small staircase hidden between two storefronts. Upstairs a cozy restaurant, dimly lit, is filled with celebrating Everest climbers. The hosts push several tables together, hobbling together a space big enough to accommodate our group, and we sit down.

Food was something that stressed me out as I prepped for this trip. For months prior, I worked with professionals to try and determine if my gut issues (the debilitating cramps I mentioned earlier, running to the bathroom sometimes as often as two or three times in the same hour) were caused by my anxiety or if they were a symptom of a bigger issue and just contributed to my mental struggle. Thus far, the feedback I received was inconclusive, leaving me feeling like I had a ticking time bomb inside of me with no idea what might set it off.

Add to this the fact that this part of the world has a reputation for causing gastro-distress in visitors, mostly because water sanitation practices are not the same as they are at home. Locals, generally, are fine to drink the water. But fragile foreigners like myself are advised to keep our mouths shut in the shower, use bottled water when brushing teeth, and to refrain from eating any raw foods that might have been washed in water. Don't get ice in your drinks and, of course, only drink bottled water.

So for dinner, I opt for easy foods that I've had before, foods I'm mostly confident won't upset my stomach: *papadum*, a paper-thin, crispy, cracker-like bread; and traditional Nepalese-style *dal bhaat*, curried chicken with black and yellow lentils served over fragrant basmati rice. I'm relieved to tuck in to the relatively familiar tastes and textures, and my relief deepens as dinner settles uneventfully in my stomach. I feel like it's a hopeful omen.

After we eat, I quickly begin to crash. My body longs for sleep, my brain aches for silence. My introverted social battery dies quickly; pair this with anxiety, and I feel myself deteriorate rapidly when I'm over-stimulated for too long. In the loud, overcrowded restaurant exacerbated by travel fatigue and dehydration, I feel myself losing my grip. All the voices start to run together, words turning incoherent. I hate having to ask, "What? I'm sorry, what?" over and over.

I think, for a second, about leaving. Making an excuse to go back to the solitary reprieve of my hotel room.

But then I think that the tigress would tough it out, so that's what I do.

Late that night I sleep fitfully, the humidity causing the coarse sheets to stick to my skin. Suddenly I hear loud booming and people screaming outside. All the careful notes my anxiety has been taking throughout the day—notes about the haphazard city infrastructure, the earthquakes, the mudslides—converge on my subconscious, and I wake up in a panic attack. I am certain, in my stupor, that the sounds are from an earthquake.

In reality, it is just New Year celebrations: fireworks, music, and revelry.

But my panic is uncontrollable. As I tremble in the hotel bed, I think, *I can't do this. I have to go home. I have to.* The tigress is gone. She has left me a shivering, sweaty mess in Kathmandu. And it occurs to me: I don't *have* to keep going. I *could* end the story. I could stop it right here.

My husband snores gently beside me, unaware of the commotion either outside the hotel or inside my head. I am disgusted with myself. He had so looked forward to this trip, but I can't keep going. It is just too much, too soon.

We can get a taxi back to the airport. We can catch a flight home as the sun rises on the first day of Hindu year 2075. But would he come back with me? In my soul I know he would, but for a minute I feel sick at the idea of him finishing the trip without me. With the blonde Australian. But my concern over this only lasts a moment before burning off under the heat of my extreme terror. I can *leave*. I can go home and stay home. I can fall back into my routine: my fear, my depression. It's not great by any means, but at least it's safe.

"Safe." A growl rumbles from a place inside my spirit that I don't recognize. "Is that really what you want?"

"Yes!" I want to scream back, but I turn the question around in my mind. What would happen after I leave? Will I wrestle with guilt for the rest of my life for having run away after my first night in Nepal? Straining to see beyond the hurricane of my panic attack, I know the answer is *yes.* I'd regret it.

I take a few deep, intentional breaths. And then I turn to my anxiety:

"I am here now, for better or worse. And I am staying. I will show up for the tour tomorrow. I will see this trip out."

My heart doesn't stop racing. I don't go back to sleep. There is no magic spell or trick to pull you out of a panic attack. But I do make a decision.

And I hear the tigress slip back into the room.

2
My Traitorous Imagination

I am glad to leave Kathmandu early the next morning.

Our group assembles in the lobby just as the sun starts to paint the world a pale grey. Everyone nibbles on protein bars and sips from water bottles, a hasty breakfast. We walk with our packs through the dirt streets to where a small passenger bus sits idling, and we load up. It's a nine-hour road trip to our next stop, and we'll be driving through mountainous terrain.

As we begin our journey, Kathmandu starts to wake up. Traffic isn't too bad yet, so I'm able to grab quick peeks into the storefronts and sidewalks of the city. Storekeepers sweep the incessant, ever-present dust from their stoops back into the street. Commuters emerge from doors nestled between storefronts and start to walk a path they know by heart. Skinny street dogs trot along the sidewalk, nose to the ground, giving pedestrians a wide berth.

The sun clears the horizon as we leave the congested confines of the city, and in the morning light, we meet a more rural side of Nepal. Our bus winds between gently sloping green hills, the preamble to the mighty Himalayas, lush with trees and plants. The hills are crisscrossed by dirt roads and studded with picturesque little buildings. Everything looks vibrant and alive.

After a few hours of driving, we pull off in front of a building sitting back from the road on the bank of the Trishuli River. Where we sit on her banks, we're almost exactly in the middle of Nepal. The Trishuli originates from a glacier in Tibet, the region just north of us, and ambles across narrow Nepal before merging with the Narayani River and, ultimately, the Ganges.

Inside the breezy, open-air building, we're met with a buffet spread of hot food: bubbling curries made with chickpeas and lentils; morsels of fried, breaded meat sprinkled with slices of green onion; steaming rice; dense golden *roti* (round flatbread).

My dad endowed me with an aversion to buffets. I can hear his voice in my head: "A buffet is only as clean as the dirtiest person to go through it." This setup, one susceptible to flies and dust from the road, makes me hesitate. But everything looks clean, and my meager breakfast didn't stick to my ribs for very long. Besides, Tim's already loaded up half a plate. I follow him and make a few careful selections.

We carry our plates down a steep staircase to an outdoor deck overlooking the sluggish, chocolatey river. Plastic chairs and tables are set up for us to eat in the shade of tall river trees. In marked contrast to the chaos of the night before, I enjoy a truly peaceful second meal in Nepal. I dare to hope that I'll find my footing on this side of the planet.

It's not long before Adnan begins to round up our group. He rises from his chair, clapping his hands on his thighs.

"Right!" He says, slightly rolling his R. He points us toward a door in the far corner of the building and encourages us to use the facilities before we get back on the road. The door leads to a steep outdoor stone staircase at the bottom of which sit two narrow, stall-shaped structures: literal outhouses.

There is no electricity, no sink, no commode. Just a hole in the wall to let in sunlight and a hole in the ground to let out . . . whatever. My first squatty potty experience.

The average American, myself included, doesn't squat a lot in their daily life, certainly not as much as the average Indian or Nepalese. Even in my short time here I've seen middle-aged women in the street squat down to sweep away litter or talk to a child as naturally as breathing. In no way do I trust my quads to be strong enough to suspend me for even ten seconds over this squatty potty. The ground is slick with wetness all around and stinks to high heaven. What if I fall? What if that wetness gets on my clothes, my skin? The stakes are too high.

Fortunately, I came prepared. Rolled up and ready in my pack is a soft silicone device shaped like an oblong funnel. It makes it possible for me to pee into the squatty potty while standing up. No squatting required. It works as advertised, and I suddenly have a deep desire to use it to write my name in snow. I now understand my younger brothers on a whole new level.

Piling back into our van, we wind our way through the Himalayan foothills on roads that used to be paved, that even had safety railings in some places. The earthquakes and mudslides from a few years ago destroyed them. Now all that remains is dusty, lane-less, pothole-riddled earth with steep inclines and drop-offs on either side. The dust is so thick at times that we lose sight of the petrol tanker in front of us.

I'm a mess of nerves in my seat and queasy with motion sickness. The Aussies are sleeping with headphones on, blissfully trusting and unaware. *What in the actual hell?* I think. *How are they fine with this?*

At one point our driver turns a corner and suddenly slams on the brakes. A semitruck carrying dry cement mix has jackknifed and over-turned in the middle of the road. It looks like a giant sea creature, beached and bleeding out. A circular hatch on top of the huge cylinder carrying the dusty contents is open. Every few seconds, a human arm flails out of the hatch, pushing cement mix into the road. The hatch is no larger than a few feet across, but a man (maybe the driver) has crawled in and is trying to offload the heavy cargo. The chaos of it all only serves to further unsettle me. I sit in my seat, spine ramrod straight with my eyes glued to the front window. Adnan is speaking to our driver in Hindi, I presume, and I wish I knew what exactly they're saying.

The road is only accessible now through a narrow space near the cab of the overturned truck, and both directions of traffic are jockeying to get through. After a lot of stop-and-go, our driver manages to pass the wreck, and we head on.

It's another seven nail-biting hours of road-tripping before we pull into Chitwan National Park. On either side of the road is deep, otherworldly forest. It makes me think of Rudyard Kipling: I imagine I can see Mowgli and Bagheera darting between the tall *sal* trees in the elephant grass.

When we are kids, we spend hours and hours in our imaginations. I think back on what would send my make-believing mind into overdrive, and I know this Nepali jungle would have been high-octane inspiration for my little brain. But so far in this magically beautiful country, my brain has only succeeded in hijacking my body with baseless panic.

At what point do our imaginations pivot and decide to exclusively generate all the reasons we don't deserve to be happy?

Growing up, I often used my imagination to develop plans. My weirdo, eleven-year-old self adored and collected floor plans for homes. I think the potential in each one was irresistible to me. As I entered middle and high school, my identity became very achievement-based because planning was fun, but the praise for a plan well executed? It was like a drug.

I carried this into my professional career, and it appeared to outsiders as initiative, drive, the ability to anticipate needs, and complete dedication to my work. I would work any hours my boss needed. I would do anything they asked, even tasks so far outside my job description that it was laughable. I never pushed back, even when I wasn't compensated for the inconvenient schedule or added responsibilities.

My supervisors were pleased. They called me their "Girl Friday," and I wore it like a sick badge, a medal I'd earned. I hoped the verbal affirmation would eventually equate to a livable wage, job security. Maybe some healthcare, that would be nice. But ultimately I wanted fulfillment. I wanted to do my best work in support of something that mattered. That's what drove me.

In reality, all those extra hours, that initiative, that drive wasn't building a stable career, nor were they building my own fulfillment. It was all building a bomb right into my very person, and every time I picked up the slack or anticipated needs or worked overtime, it brought that bomb closer to detonating.

Let me set the scene of my mindset at the time: The company I work for has very old-school management. It's fear-based, condescending, and manipulative. My bosses view the idea of cultivating passion, community, and a healthy work/life balance for employees as counterproductive. Maybe even dangerous. Your paycheck is expected to be your ultimate fulfillment, and expecting anything more out of your job is expecting too much.

Out of this blooms a cancerous culture of scarcity. Gossip is rampant. Employees never really know where they stand in the minds of their employer. Every phone call, every meeting could be a trap. I've seen an employee get reamed out about something like punctuality, only for the lecturing manager to be a no-show at their very next meeting with that same berated employee. Hoarding work or working overtime is common because it gives us underlings at least a small sense of job security.

I'm ashamed to admit it, but I rarely rise above the toxic culture. I almost always participate in this economy of misery: receiving abuse to then dole it out myself. With my off-hours trauma struggles, I tell myself, there's just not enough fight left in me. But I know that's not true because as soon as I'm trapped in a contentious meeting, I'm all sneers and scoffs and fists.

At some point I looked in the mirror and realized the bomb had exploded. I was scared, helpless, and ashamed because I didn't recognize the person staring back at me.

The bomb was built with assumptions and rationalizations I wasn't always aware of. I worked from the premise that if I was perfect (better than perfect) and made all the right calls, I could determine both my self-worth and my future. I could lock in my security, my status, and a sunshiney existence all based on my performance. But this has never, ever been true.

Realizing this was like falling through pond ice, and it got tangled up in my recovery after the Breaking. The two revelations weren't dissimilar.

In both situations I did everything I was supposed to do to prevent a terrible outcome.

I followed instructions.

I went above and beyond.

I played by all the rules and did all the extra credit assignments.

And yet, something completely outside of my control—an overbearing, toxic work environment in one instance, the regrettable choices of another person in the other—superseded everything I'd done and left me shattered.

How is that fair?

And what happens when you do everything to make the grade, but factors outside of your control ensure your failure? What happens when you do everything in your power to prevent trauma or relational distress or tragedy, and it happens anyway?

Anxiety happens. To regain some sense of control, Anxiety steps in and suggests that maybe she can help prevent this from happening again. In return, she simply requires all your imagination and all your creativity, which she will use to predict every possible worst-case scenario. That way, at least, you'll see it coming.

Anxiety takes the imagination we once used to explore our own endless potential and turns it into a self-sabotaging conspiracy theory machine.

PTSD-related anxiety, like mine, is just regular anxiety with a folder full of evidence under her arm. She has proof that it will all hit the fan at some point, so you're better off giving her the keys and letting her drive. It is exponentially harder to deny her the driver's seat.

I had high hopes for this trip. I hoped that it would maybe help me find my way to the confident, healed, anxiety-impervious person I want to be. But last night reinforced that I'm still susceptible to its folder of evidence.

I'm pulled away from my thoughts as our van finally arrives at our hotel in Chitwan. It's a beautifully manicured compound of six buildings spread out on a walled property. Dusty footpaths winding through luscious landscaping connect the architecture. Kathmandu was urban, dizzying, and incessantly loud, but this is a jungle paradise, slow and intentional. Much more my speed.

Our first morning I'm fully awake as the sun chases away the night with its soft light. This is one of my favorite things about traveling: it can turn this night owl into a temporary early bird.

When the breeze pushes through our screen windows, it smells like mosquito coils and gardenia. A symphony of faint chirps starts, each one an invitation to continue following the tigress. But in the cool light of morning made softer by the sweeping mosquito net hanging over our bed, I'm fine to stay put a while and listen to the jungle.

Tim rolls over beside me, and I can just make out his face, his dirty blond curls made messy with sleep. I seem to feel more than I can see his blue eyes open and search for mine.

Sometimes (too often) I forget that he's recovering from his own trauma too. In the early weeks following the Breaking, it felt like the Himalayas lay between us. We barely spoke. We didn't touch, we didn't kiss. I stayed on my side of the bed. It was what I needed then, that space. But everything that has a cause also has an effect. And Tim was deeply affected by my inward draw, that loss of the clear-eyed bride he married.

We went to couple's therapy in the early days, when the shock was still scalding hot. Tim searched for a Christian couple's therapist because that was all he could think to do. We found one. It was a man, short, balding, and soft-spoken, who took our insurance. The first few sessions were okay, but something recoiled in me when he started calling me "my little sister" while still calling Tim by his name. When the therapist started making comments about how he disliked women "bossing him around," I felt the barriers around my soul slam shut completely. Tim felt it too, felt me pull away, and canceled all our future appointments.

Partners of trauma victims are also victims, victims of what's called secondary trauma. But it can be hard for them to pursue the healing they need when they're wrapped up in supporting their person. It's not uncommon for partners to reach a point of burnout, especially if the primary trauma victim is not working to heal. Supporting someone who has no interest in healing can become incredibly taxing for a partner. Not long after our attempt at couple's therapy, I started with my own individual therapist. She was a woman the age of my mom; she was tender but took no shit. She was just what I needed, and I've fought hard for my healing since then. But I still wonder if Tim has ever experienced that point of burnout, and I am suddenly awash in relief that I did not call off our trip last night in Kathmandu.

How exhaustive it must be to consistently support a limping partner. How difficult to constantly ride the unpredictable breakers of their emotions and shifting thoughts, to make all the decisions and bear the weight of obligations they themselves can't shoulder. Not all partners can manage it. Not all partners try. Not all partners are like Tim.

I feel Tim's gaze searching my face, and I know he's looking for any signs of repeat terror like the kind that found me in Kathmandu. He's only been awake for a few seconds and already he's orienting himself to me. I close the space between us and let him know this is a new, more clear-eyed morning.

Leaving our room, we make our way along a dusty path to the open-air cabana where breakfast waits for us. We put jungle flower honey in our coffee, and after several days without coffee altogether, it's life-giving. Definitely different, but still wholly resurrecting.

Our group then ventures out on a safari day trip, making the ten-minute walk from our hotel to the Rapti River. On the opposite shore, Jurassic-sized crocodiles sunbathe. Just behind them lies the wild jungle. It's protected land, watched over by the army, and home to storybook wildlife, including several endangered species.

The crocodiles are still in sight as we cross the river in shallow dugout canoes and climb into jeeps on the opposite bank. I imagine I look ridiculous. I'm wearing long, baggy harem pants, a long-sleeved jacket, a gauzy scarf, and a wide-brimmed hat. It's almost one hundred degrees Fahrenheit, but here's the thing about me: I always get sunburned. I have over a week of traveling ahead of me, and I don't want to fry this early in our schedule.

During our six-hour excursion, our safari guide, Suk, points left and right, spotting wildlife. We meet *chital*, small spotted deer unbothered by our noisy jeeps. We also see rhinos finding refuge from the intense sun in muddy water and elephants grazing along the jungle tree line and, of course, a few cheeky monkeys looking to swipe unattended items at military outposts.

There is a bird whose call sounds like someone laughing hysterically. It cracks me up every time I hear it, but I can't figure out what it is. Every time I ask our guide to name it, it stops singing.

After several hours in the jungle, we cross back to the other side of the river and walk a short distance to an outdoor restaurant without a roof or walls. We sit outside on the riverbank in plastic chairs whose synthetic colors have gone tender with time.

"Once," Adnan says as he points to the walkway between the tables, "a tiger walked right through here."

I slip off my sandals and snuggle my feet into the riverbank sand that has absorbed the warmth of the sun all day. Our server brings us bottled water, curry, spicy steamed chicken-stuffed dumplings called *momos*, fluffy tandoori roti flatbread, and bottles of Everest—a blonde Nepali ale. Between courses, we spot a sambar stag, the tiger's favorite meal, hiding in the tall grass on the other side of the river. The sun, a big tangerine ball in the sky, slips below the tree line, and the night lets down her hair around us.

3
Suffering

"Life is suffering."

Adnan is smiling wide at my slack-jawed expression, bobbling his head side to side and making the OK sign with both hands as he recites the Buddhist/Hindu saying. This isn't the first time he's used it.

He first said it during the perilous road trip from Kathmandu to Chitwan, and he said it again on the circuitous journey from Chitwan to our next destination in Lumbini: the birthplace of Buddha. It took us a few hours by car to get here, and we arrive in the heat of the day. He also said it when we found out the Internet cable at our Lumbini hotel had been accidentally cut, rendering our stay WiFi-less. The saying, it seems, applies to all kinds of suffering.

Adnan gives us a crash course on Buddhism as we trek from the parking lot to the heart of the sacred grounds spread around the roots of an enormous tree. It's about 105 degrees Fahrenheit with high humidity, making it hard for me to concentrate. I forget what it feels like not to be sweaty. I'm sweating in places I didn't even know I could sweat. Do knees normally sweat?

I force myself to clue in to what Adnan is saying. Around the fifth or sixth centuries BCE, he tells us, Queen Maya of Shakya gave birth to a son, Gautama Buddha, while gripping the branch of a sal tree for support. After renouncing his royal status, Gautama Buddha spent his life meditating, refusing sensual pleasures, and teaching as he traveled around the continent gradually creating a monastic order.

"He would later die under the same type of tree he was born under," Adnan explains, highlighting how these two symmetrical events forever made the sal tree significant to both the Hindu and Buddhist faiths. Sal trees blossom but ever so briefly, additionally rendering them a Buddhist symbol of the transient nature of all good things. My depression is totally down with this concept, nodding and snapping her fingers like a hipster, saying, "Nothing. Good. Lasts."

Adnan shows us where to leave our shoes at the gate of the memorial grounds. He explains that we will need to walk to and around the temple barefoot because this is holy ground. Our shoes will be waiting for us when we're done. The heat radiates off the pavement in shimmering ripples, and the temple is not a short walk from the shoe stand. That's when he says it for the fourth time: "Life is suffering."

Initially this phrase put me off. It smacked of abdication or a shirking of responsibility. I think this aversion was partially due to my American heritage; our national identity pivots around being the hero, and we tie our worth to what we do. We so value action.

On the other hand, I think back to yesterday when we drove by huge Nepali brick kilns where people labored in the already-sweltering sun. They wound their way among acres of bricks piled around a single smokestack rising like Tolkien's Barad-dûr. I even saw kids in these brickyards. Because of my familiarity with the work of the International Justice Mission, I knew these remote brick kilns sometimes conceal modern-day slaves. To me, in the face of that, "Life is suffering" seems a minimization of injustice.

I also think some of my aversion to the mantra was influenced by the fact that the church doesn't really sit in suffering. Not in my experience, at least. The church rushes. It rushes through Good Friday to get to Easter Sunday. Rushes through the pain to get to the biblical promise that God works all things together for the good of those who love him. It's so much easier to sit in celebration than in struggle. The resurrected Jesus (triumphant, in control, and shiny) is preferred over the Gethsemane Jesus (broken, terrified, and bloody). And in all that rushing toward the empty tomb, people are left behind in the garden of grief. I certainly felt left behind.

After the Breaking I struggled in a sea of smiley Christians all rushing toward celebration while I desperately tried to keep my head above the waves. I tried rushing myself, I tried to expedite my grief, thinking maybe the problem was me. But I couldn't get there. Couldn't find the happily ever after. Many times, in the words of Lin-Manuel Miranda, I was in so deep it felt like it would be easier to just swim down.

And it didn't make sense to me. Growing up in the evangelical church, I heard people speak countless times about how they experienced "peace beyond understanding" or "God's presence" in their moments of crisis. I'm happy for them, but all I felt in the midst of my Breaking was abandonment. I can't help but wonder: did they *really* feel peace as their marriage dissolved? As they buried their child? As their lives crumbled around them?

Or were they rushed, like I felt I was?

I only told a handful of people about my own Breaking, hiding and cradling my wound like an injured animal. Most of those (well-meaning) people gave me rushing, reductionist, Christian buzzwords and platitudes:

"You can't be angry at God about this."

"We just have to trust that God has a plan."

"Make sure you don't neglect your quiet times in this season."

"God works all things together for the good of those who love him."

It was like sand in an open wound. It burned and it was abrasive and it did nothing to validate or bear witness to my suffering. It made me angry because, deep down, I felt like this God they were foisting on me—this absent, indifferent entity—was the one who had lured me into a boxing ring to face an opponent I had never agreed to fight.

That is, if God was even there at all.

In my darkest moments I curled up not in a sanctuary and not in scripture, but inside the confessions of my fellow sufferers. I loved a podcast called *Terrible, Thanks for Asking* where the host Nora McInerny and her guests look closely at hard things they've experienced, things like death, sickness, and abuse. Often I listened as complete strangers gave words to my suffering and explained my charred insides to me:

> "Time does not heal all wounds. That's just something that people like to stitch on pillows . . . . Time is irrelevant to this kind of pain."
>
> "We don't get to pick what wrecks us, what changes us. We don't get to pick what it is or when it happens."
>
> "We are allowed to hold our own experiences up to the light and decide what to call it, to define it for ourselves, and explain that meaning to the people around us."
>
> "It's okay to not be okay."

This was tremendously healing for me. Most of the time I quite literally had no words with which to frame my experiences. Hearing others verbalize their own anguish was like suddenly having a blindfold removed. Not only could I better understand myself, but I could see a way forward, even if it was only a few steps. And all this came not from self-help or scripture or a scrappy "hurry-and-fix-it" mentality. Just from affirming a shared pain.

One of the biggest obstacles that kept me from seeking professional therapy was that I didn't want someone "fixing" it. I felt like I was bleeding out, and I thought going to therapy would just add someone explaining tourniquet theory to my situation. But, in my very first session, after I spent twenty minutes ugly-crying and word-vomiting all over a lady I'd just met, she simply said, "You have been carrying so much." I exhaled after holding my breath for six months.

It's what made me realize that this is where we have to start: life is suffering. It's hard and so utterly unfair, and people like me and you are carrying it all. I see you. It's okay to not be okay.

As I walk with dozens of other visitors toward the temple, all of us on burning feet, I'm reminded that we have a responsibility to walk with people dealing with hard things and bear witness to their suffering. We might want to rush, fix it immediately, and get to the celebration, the "after" picture, the happy ending. That's much easier than acknowledging that life is so often suffering. But more often than not, we need to sit on our hands and simply affirm their pain.

Zigzagging in the fields around the temple are the foundations of ancient monasteries that were built here for pilgrims as early as the third century BCE. The low, haphazard brick walls are proof of a devotion that spans two millennia.

The actual birthplace of Buddha is protected by a modest white temple. It takes no time to walk through, and soon we exit back out into the sun and the Sacred Garden. Quick-stepping from shadow to shadow, our group settles beneath the arms of the ancient tree covered in *lungta* prayer flags.

Lungta flags are made of five differently colored square cloths strung together with twine that, I later learn, have Buddhist sutras written on them. I've seen them everywhere in Nepal and even bought myself a small banner of them to bring home. The colors represent the elements: white is air, blue is sky or space, yellow is earth, green is water, and red is fire. They spread their blessings on the wind as it brushes past; the Sacred Garden is covered in them. They softly flap overhead as we walk the dappled ground, our feet thankful for the shade. Before we go, Tim lights an incense stick and places it on the memorial shrine nestled at the base of the huge tree.

Back at the hotel our team convenes in the dining room just off the lobby. The menu offers the same foods we've seen in Chitwan and Kathmandu: *chapati*, *biryani*, lentils, rice. But the waitstaff is also pushing the fresh salads and produce they have available, just for us. I look at Adnan tentatively, and he explains that they have washed the raw salad components in iodine (instead of potentially contaminated water) to make them safe for us to eat.

Every experience I've ever had with iodine floods my brain, and in no way is my appetite piqued. I remember my childhood best friend using it on her foot after having surgery on an ingrown toenail. I remember in high school filling my cupped palm with the dark, metallic-smelling liquid and gently applying it to the still-raw belly button of our newborn foal as she wobbled after her mom in the little birthing paddock beside our farmhouse. My hands were stained for days.

I'm desperate for a crisp, cool salad. But not that desperate.

I opt instead to try something called *paneer*. Paneer is a soft, mild, white cheese that's usually seasoned and served in big chunks. Adnan says it's made from water buffalo milk. That's definitely a new one, but I hardly ever meet a cheese I don't like, and dairy has never given my temperamental stomach a problem. I give it a try.

And I am blessed. Although it's a soft cheese, it doesn't melt easily, so it's a great addition to bubbling curries or just wrapped in chapati. It would soon become one of my staples while in India.

Later that night, after we're full of cheese and chapati, Tim and I wash off our feet and hours of sweat in cool showers and fall asleep watching Indian TV from the hazy embrace of our hanging mosquito net.

It's morning, and we're back on the bus well before sunrise. Today we face one of our longest drives—ten hours total. The plan is to cross over the border early and finally introduce ourselves to India. We won't stop until we reach Varanasi about 220 miles away.

We've just left Lumbini, which sits quite close to the national border, so we won't have to wait long before entering India. As we speed ever closer, we pass dozens—hundreds—of idling semis and dump trucks. They're lined up one after the other in the far left lane for what seems like miles. We zoom past them in the right-hand lane. Adnan explains that the customs process for importing into India is time-consuming and what we're seeing is the backlog.

"What do the drivers do?" I wonder aloud, eyeing the empty, dry land stretching away across the horizon. Adnan shrugs and says, "They must wait, often for days."

Buildings grow in our windshield, and soon our van rumbles to a stop. Our Nepalese driver won't be taking us the rest of the way; an

Indian driver with another van will be waiting on the other side of the border. We gather our stuff and disembark.

Our group walks a short distance to an understated building, a small banner reading "Immigration, India" stretched across its face. A garland of old, dried marigolds, most of which have long since rotted off the string, drapes under the banner. It's a little underwhelming. But once we fill out our immigration forms by hand and show the attendant our travel visas, we walk out onto Indian soil. It's a magical feeling.

About two hours into India, our van's AC gives out. We keep driving; there's nothing we can do about it. Most of the group tries to nap under the weight of the unrelenting heat. Their trust and surrender amazes me. I can't sleep, I can barely breathe. The anxiety that found me that first night in Kathmandu is still very much present, bubbling and writhing just below the surface.

When the driver says we are three hours away from the border, my phone says it is 106 degrees. Adnan turns to me and says, with his rhythmically rolled Rs, "I feel like a roast chicken."

I smile. "Me too." Then I bobble my head side to side, touch the tips of my pointer fingers to the tips of their neighboring thumbs, make two Buddha hands, and say, "Life is suffering."

4
Beside the Ganges

Varanasi is a tightly woven tapestry of the ancient and the sacred. The asphalt streets reflect this. They are haphazard and cracked, snaking between buildings and littered with trash, standing water, and feces. As the oldest continually occupied city in the world, it's an urban lasagna: layer on layer on layer of city.

Our first morning we set out early to try and beat the heat. At 8:00 AM it's already one hundred degrees, but even that won't stop me from having a piping hot chai over breakfast. I forgo my typical coffee to try this quintessential taste of India, and after those first few sips, it tastes so good that I vow never to go back to my usual caffeine routine. Not while I'm here, at least. It's completely different from the chai I've experienced in the States: it's deeply creamy (Adnan tells me this is because they make it with water buffalo milk) with punchy spices that tingle all the way up my nose and down my throat. It tastes like a bonfire. It tastes like courage. My tongue burns after each sip, and I genuinely can't tell if it's because of the spices or the temperature of the silky, amber liquid.

After breakfast we pile into motorized *rickshaws* and zip into the street. Traffic here would be intense anyway, with hundreds of pedestrians playing Frogger, incessant horn-blowing, and nonexistent lanes, but add lumbering, one-ton cows to the mix, and it feels like absolute chaos.

It doesn't even phase our particular driver. He takes us as far into the city as he can. However, because portions of the city were built before motorized vehicles existed, some streets are off-limits to engines.

Tim and I hop into a bike-towed rickshaw, and an older man who probably weighs 150 pounds peddles us through traffic like it's nothing. He, too, can only take us so far because, like motorized vehicles, bicycles are not allowed in the city's oldest parts. From here we must walk.

Our group winds single-file through alleyways that are older than my home country. Colorful tarps and fabric stretched overhead between walls afford us some shade and dye the sunlight in blues and oranges. Bollywood music, blaring from an unseen source, clips and garbles. It bounces off walls covered in decades of graffiti and painted advertisements.

Adnan leads us to a large opening in an alley wall where a barefoot man sits cross-legged with a large silver mixing bowl in his lap. Around his perch are bunches of bananas, mangos, and jars of dried fruits and spices. Behind him is a small, high-ceilinged room filled with mismatched chairs. A fan whirs overhead.

"Who would care for *lassi?*" asks Adnan.

Lassi is a dairy-based dessert beverage not unlike yogurt that can be flavored and topped with whatever goodies you like. I decline. Something about dairy-based street food makes me anxious, mostly because I don't see any refrigeration machinery anywhere. I like my lassi super cold and super safe. Life is suffering, sure, I'm willing to affirm that, but that doesn't mean I'm going to seek suffering out. We still have days of travel ahead of us and a tight schedule. I'm not going to risk getting sick.

Looking back at this moment, it's easy to see that the conclusions I'd accepted in my head pushing past fear and anxiety were still working their way out of the grey matter between my ears and into my choices. I didn't know it then, but I'd get another shot at street lassi in a different Indian city soon.

Most people in our group place orders, including Tim, who selects a sweet saffron lassi, and we sit down inside the little room. As our eyes adjust to the dark interior, we notice there are little square passport photos covering the high walls. Hundreds of faces look back at us. Some pictures are old and faded, the corners curling away from the wall. Some aren't even photos but hand-drawn self-portraits on scraps of paper added by those who wanted to participate but were unprepared.

By some strange coincidence Tim happens to have a copy of both our passport photos in his pocket. The passport photo service we used issued our prints in sets of four; one was needed for the Nepal visa application, two for the India visa application. Tim had stuck the last lonely squares between the pages of his passport. Just in case.

We add our faces to the mosaic of memories inside the shop just as his lassi is served to him in a little red clay pot. When he finishes, the barefooted man mimes instructions on where to put the empty pot.

"You can throw it into the gutter," translates Adnan. "It's cheaper and safer for them to use these clay pots instead of plastic cups." Looking at the street's edges, we notice that there are hundreds of red shards from previous patrons. Like a kid who's just been taught to spit, Tim gleefully obeys, and the pot shatters. We resume our trek through old Varanasi.

Suddenly we turn a corner, and there she is, glistening in the sun: the River Ganges.

She is stunning. A National Geographic feature Tim and I watched prior to our trip told us that hundreds of Hindus trek to her banks every day to bathe in the holy water and wash their sins away. "She is a Hindu goddess," the voice-over said reverently, "a watery ribbon springing from the hair of Shiva and flowing through heaven, earth, and the nether-world." On a strictly factual level, however, she is disturbingly polluted. I found a study online that stated the level of fecal coliform bacteria from human waste in the water is more than 100 times the government's official limit, and this stat was published ten years before we ever stepped foot in the country. The river doesn't appear to have gotten any cleaner since then. The endangered Ganges Dolphin, unique to this part of the world, is nearly extinct because of this unchecked pollution.

But as we walk along the riverside *ghats*, massive stairs along the river's edge, people are swimming, bathing, doing laundry, and collecting the holy water in plastic containers to anoint their homes and shrines. Honestly, the heat is so intense, with no shade anywhere, I begin to envy those splashing around in the dark waves.

The Ganges' depth fluctuates dramatically. Adnan tells us that during the rainy season she can rise twenty feet or more, so the ghats were built to give people access to the water regardless of its height. After the rainy season, when the water retracts, the ghats are covered in mud and refuse, so they are cleaned every year.

Adnan leads us from one ghat to another. We pass stray goats, shirtless kids, and religious men, their faces smeared white with ash, their bodies wrapped in bright orange cloth. They call out, reaching toward us, attempting to bestow a blessing or prophecy in exchange for cash.

Adnan suddenly turns to huddle us all in close to him. "Around this next corner," he says in a hushed, reverent voice, "is a place where the burning happens. Please do not take pictures. It is a very sacred place. We must be respectful."

The air is heavy with the smell of woodsmoke as he leads on. My stomach knots up. I knew this was coming, of course. I knew when we booked this trip that our time in Varanasi would include this next experience. Varanasi is, after all, a place where people live side by side with death, and all the rites and rituals that come with it.

Hindus believe that if your body is surrendered to the Ganges after your death, you go straight to heaven, Adnan explains. Some bodies are simply placed into the water. But most are cremated on the banks of the holy river, their ashes pushed into the water to release the deceased into the arms of heaven. We're about to walk into one of these areas used for cremation.

I'd chosen not to think too hard about seeing all this up close and in-person. I kicked the can down the road until the very last minute, which is now, and even still, my brain feels numb. Like it's insulating itself from this very intimate encounter with something that's haunted me, day and night, since my Breaking.

I'd never had a fear of death, but after my Breaking, I was consumed by it. My thoughts constantly fixated on it in the dark moments, the quiet hours of the night. And while this lessened over time, it never went away. Like a floater in my eye, death was always there, and even when I wasn't paying attention to it, it impacted how I saw the world.

To be clear, I was not suicidal. On the contrary, I was desperately afraid of my own end. I couldn't sleep on my back because inevitably my mind would whisper, "The way your bones are aligned now? Spine straight, hands stacked over sternum. That's how they'll be when you're put in the ground." Even in happy moments my brain would suddenly shove my heart into a blender with thoughts like, *Is this your last birthday? The last time you'll see your sister? Is this the last time you'll make love with Tim?*

My faith had informed all my understandings of death and whatever comes after it. But my faith had been shattered, and it left behind a great, gaping nothingness. Depression's icy voice took over, and I trembled in the face of the void, the emptiness, the finality of it.

As we round the corner, we pass a stone bench with a sleeping street dog curled up tightly in its scant noon shadow. Every rib is visible under its patchy skin. I watch it as I walk by, waiting for its eyes to open and take stock of the humans disrupting its nap.

Then I realize it's not sleeping. It's dead. A fitting sentry for the "place where the burning happens."

How did it know? Could it smell death on the air and knew this was where it must come when its time was through?

The burning place is a large semicircle pit next to this portion of the river. It's a couple hundred feet long, built down into the stone ghat. Everything is black with smoke and soot. The walls, the ground, the workers are all covered in it. They tend large funeral pyres fed by logs thicker than my waist. I order my eyes not to look too hard at the flickering cloth mounds at the base of the flames. The fires, Adnan tells us later, never stop burning. Twenty-four hours a day, every single day of the year. They never go hungry.

As we slowly make our way around the burning area, the sound of chanting grows. A group of people approaches, ornamented with scarves of strung marigolds and ceremonial sweeps of white ash and gold paste made from turmeric on their faces. On their shoulders they carry a stretcher. And on that stretcher is another body, white-cloth wrapped and adorned with marigolds and gold jewelry. They pass right by us.

My family is from the deep south of America, from a culture whose mourning rituals feature open caskets, embalmed faces, and hours of visitation, so the bodies around me now, on the stretcher and on the pyres, are not the first I've ever seen. I was well into adulthood before I learned that my experience is not the norm everywhere in America, where urns filled with ashes or closed caskets are more typical. At visitations in the south, people could, and often did, reach out and touch their loved ones who had passed on. I remember watching attendees pat the deceased's hands, adjust their collar, or fix their hair.

The first time I saw a body, I was caught somewhere between childhood and womanhood. It's a weird time to first experience death, to see your parents grieve deeply while trying to wrap your own mind around the never-see-them-again. My great-grandfather said he wanted to be buried in a goofy tie, a final wink to his great-grandkids, of whom I was the oldest. The image of his body lying there looking nothing like him, wearing that tie with Kermit, Fozzie Bear, and the gang grinning up at me, is burned into my brain.

I know it was a gesture rooted in love, but I'm still not sure how I feel about it. A person's first brush with death is unnerving even without the Muppets in the mix. It feels surreal to be standing now on the periphery of mourning families performing rituals so different, and yet not, from the ones I know.

But my thoughts, I'm surprised to notice, are not preoccupied with the idea of my own death like they have so often been this past year. I'm thinking instead of the living. The family. The friends. The ones left behind to sweep away the ashes of their loved ones not once, but over and over and over again. If we're lucky enough to love someone, but unlucky enough to lose them, we'll be saying goodbye to them for the rest of our lives.

When we hear their favorite song and feel that hot rush of tears, we sweep their ashes into the river again.

When we eat their favorite food and it turns tasteless in their absence, we bury them again.

Every holiday and anniversary.

Every time we reach for our phone to text them.

Every time we think, *I wish they were here, they would've loved this.*

It's an impossible thing we do: carrying on after the finality of death.

Turning away from the chanting grievers, my tour group makes its way back toward the heart of the city. As we move into the relative cool of a shaded alleyway, I can still smell the woodsmoke that clings to my clothes, my hair, my skin.

———————

Our hotel, Surya Kaiser, is built close to the shore of the river. It's a gorgeous, multi-story white palace with manicured grounds and an expansive courtyard. Originally built in 1818 for a Nepalese king, it now serves as a banquet hall for weddings and accommodations for tourists like us.

We convene in the dining room to eat dinner before our evening excursion. Tim and I order a sweet lime soda, and it quickly becomes our new favorite chilled drink. It's exactly what it sounds like: lime juice, soda water, and sugar. You can order it with salt instead of sugar, at which point it's basically a bubbly electrolyte. But sweet is the way to go.

For our meal, Tim and I elect to try something new, something called *angoori kofta*: spinach and cheese dumplings stuffed with heat-softened nuts and golden raisins, swimming in a gravy made from tomatoes and blended cashews. Most importantly, it's served steaming hot and doesn't flaunt any intimidating ingredients that might upset my stomach. It is every bit as satisfying as it sounds.

Afterward, we hail a handful of rickshaws and head back out into the city. It's just as busy as it was during the day. I wonder if there's ever a time when these streets are clear, or at least clearer, and slower—it seems like India only has one speed.

We make our way through the crowds and back into the oldest part of Varanasi, the part that sidles up alongside the Ganges. Our group follows Adnan down to the very lip of the water and boards a sun-bleached wooden boat. Every night on the Ganges' shores there is a massive ceremony for the deceased Hindus who were cremated that day. It's why we've come back: we're attending.

Viewing the shore from the middle of the river, we can better see the enormous ghats and riverside palaces built centuries ago by wealthy or royal Hindus in preparation for their deaths. We can also see smaller cremation fires blazing onshore for those who could not (or didn't want to) be cremated on the official pyres we saw earlier. Our boat reaches the ceremony site and joins dozens of others filled with mourners. They pack together so closely that kids selling postcards, hot chai, and cold water can walk across one and step onto the next in the dark. The air smells like smoke and dirty water as the holy men begin performing the rites.

I notice two Indian women staring at me from the boat just in front of ours. Their bodies are turned in toward each other, faces fixed on me. On the first night in Kathmandu, Adnan had warned our group that people would stare at us, ask for selfies with us, even thrust their babies into our arms, this last motivated by a charming mix of parental pride, warm hospitality, and a hope that a fascinating foreigner might bring their child a little good luck. He was right, but I'm still not quite used to it. I meet the women's gaze a few times and quickly look away. They keep staring.

Ever since the Breaking, I greatly feared intimacy with anyone. Sometimes even eye contact felt like a dangerous level of closeness to me. I felt that my trauma story was somehow spelled out in my eyes and all it would take for someone to discover it would be for them to look at me long enough. Then they'd know. They would see my failure, my humiliation, my inability to recover . . .

And I couldn't take any more outside input. I'd opened up a few times to people around me, and I feared that if I dared to let myself be seen again, if I put down my guard and let my eyes speak, I'd just get more of the same dismissive, bumper-sticker answers that were so abrasive to my raw soul.

So I hid behind my lashes while I spoke to people. I would pick at my nails. I would check my phone. Only when other people were speaking, when their attentions were on themselves and their own words, would I meet their eyes. It was the smallest scrap of control, the most I could find in a season where I felt very much out of control, and I seized it.

My eye contact aversion wasn't only rooted in self-preservation and control. My soul had become a Pandora's box of dark thoughts and messy emotions all tumbling over themselves: deep grief melded with jaded doubt and despair, punctuated by frenetic anxiety and panic, and sustained by an ever-present undercurrent of molten rage. In the words of Chris Mc Geown, "There were two reasons I was scared to let people in; the damage they could do, and the damage they could find." I feared that if I opened the floodgates to those closest to me, I might explode all over them, unintentionally making them feel like the target of my anguish. Worse, I worried I would pull them down with me. I remembered Sunday school lessons that likened doubt to a weed, an insidious, invasive species that would choke out the lovelier plants if given the tiniest toehold, and I would rather suffer a dozen times over than plant the seeds of doubt and despair in the heart of someone I cared about. This is an experience I wish on no one.

With those unhelpful ideas from Sunday school thrown in, I was further isolated from my anxiety. I locked myself away. And in locking myself away, it became very difficult to be a good wife, friend, sister, human.

I would learn how to overcome this. It would take years, but I would relearn how to look someone in the eye and own the space I took up. To root myself in the moment. Eventually I would chronicle this story for others. For you. But there was work I had to do first.

Because intimacy is vulnerability. It takes tremendous courage to show up and be available to those around you, just as you are. You risk rejection. You risk being snubbed. You risk being misunderstood. You risk being judged and being shamed.

These are significant risks. Maybe that's the whole point of Jesus. Even with all my complicated emotions and conflicted perceptions about God, I can't help but like that Nazarene carpenter who showed up under the banner of "God with us."

Not God omniscient.

Not God omnipotent.

Not God of the megachurches and prosperity gospel and GOP.

Just . . . with us. Present. Here. Together.

As I float on the Ganges, the holy Hindu men and the *chaiwallahs* (tea sellers) shouting their respective chants, I risk one more glance at the two women in front of me.

They are still staring, bold and unblinking.

We meet each other's gaze, but I don't look away this time. I anchor myself to the moment and try to just . . . be here. Open and present. I risk a smile and a small head wobble.

Both their faces blossom into big warm smiles, earnest head wobbles back. They bring their hands in prayer position to their foreheads and bow in my direction. The physical gesture of *namaste*. Translated literally, it means, "I acknowledge the divinity within you."

Intimacy requires significant risk, but this great risk creates the space needed for great gain. To be seen as you are and be received into the arms of humanity—this is one of the most divine, "of God" experiences.

If God is there and if God is good, then surely God has given us to one another. And what a magnificent, terrifying, overwhelming, complicated, beautiful gift.

I feel, at this moment on the Ganges, that these two women sitting in a sun-bleached rowboat are ambassadors. They are simply watching me, as the universe watches each of us, their eyes asking: *Are you going to keep looking at your shoes, arrested by the thought of risk? Afraid to see and be seen?*

I hope you look up, frightening as it may be. I hope you see the divinity inside yourself and your fellow humans. And I hope you let yourself be seen, because you are enough, just as you are. Even in your struggle and your becoming. You are enough.

We are waiting for you.

Before our boat returns to shore, Tim and I light small candles held afloat in bowls made of sal leaves and release them, with a prayer, into the ripples of the Ganges.

5
White-Hot Grief

The following day we prepare to leave Varanasi and head to Agra and the much-anticipated Taj Mahal. And I'm utterly sick. I spent most of the night on the toilet or curled over my knees in agony. What started as mild cramps intensified into extreme pain. I got to the point where I felt nauseous, and I wasn't sure if it was because of the white-hot abdominal pain or because I truly needed to vomit. The only thing that kept me from crying out and waking Tim was deep, intentional breaths.

Is it weird? This aversion I have to enlisting help when I'm panicking in Kathmandu or coming down with an intense illness in Varanasi? I don't know, I can't analyze that right now. I'm just trying to self-soothe.

In the morning the cramps and nausea still won't let up. Ever since leaving Kathmandu, I haven't had any significant anxiety attacks, so I don't feel like anxiety is the root of the problem. I grind my teeth in frustration as I remember that yesterday there were diced raw onions and cilantro leaves on the *chole* I ate. Chole is an Indian breakfast dish made of chickpeas and masala spices. It's wonderful: flavorful but mild, filling without being heavy. And it would've been perfect for my sensitive gut had it not been for those few little garnishes.

This couldn't have come at a worse time: we plan to travel to Agra by overnight sleeper train. Tim and I tried this once between London and Edinburgh, and even with the train's modern, first-world flair, it was not fun. Gentle rocking? Quiet, constant percussion from the tracks? That's what I imagined it would be like to sleep on a train. In reality, I slept very little. The rocking: not gentle, but rough and unpredictable. The percussion: I couldn't even hear it over our loud neighbors and the fire alarm going off twice. I'm the type of person who needs my sleep, so I'm not sure why I thought that trying a sleeper train Indian-style would be a good idea.

Tim prepares for the journey by getting a massage. This was supposed to be a couple's massage, but I decline. Two things that don't ever mix well are massages and diarrhea.

I spend every minute I can in the bathroom, literally until the moment they load the *tuk-tuks* with our group's luggage. On our way to the train station the tuk-tuk zigzags through traffic while I clutch my abdomen, my eyes screwed shut, my knee jumping up and down in a desperate attempt to self-soothe. I repeat bathroom-related affirmations over myself:

> *You're prepared.*
> *You just spent the entire morning in the bathroom.*
> *And there will be a bathroom on the train.*
> *Even if you have to camp out inside it, even if you're bombing into a hole in the train's floor, you'll be alright. You'll make it to Agra.*
> *You've got this, tiger.*

Even the tigress is sick. That's how intense gastrointestinal distress is: it will reach through your psyche and infect your alter ego. Now that I'm thinking about it, in *Life of Pi* seasickness was the same way. When Pi was sick, so was the tiger.

When we arrive at Varanasi Junction, I carefully hoist my backpack onto my shoulders and join a throng of people headed toward the rails. The train station is a large, open structure situated off a major intersection. Traffic kicks up hot dust that makes my eyes itch and sticks to my sweaty skin as we walk toward the turnstiles that block the entrance of the cement building. Inside, we find ourselves standing on an elevated balcony overlooking the rest of the station. Stairs lead to walkways that straddle the rails or down to various platforms where dozens and dozens of people sit on the floor, waiting for their trains.

I decided to wear my leggings on this one day. They're my go-to back home, but the tour company encouraged us not to wear tight-fitting pants or leggings as it's not common clothing for women in India. But I'm about to sleep on a train. If I'm going to be in the same clothes for hours and hours, I'm going to be comfortable. I can feel people's eyes on me as I walk down the steps and through the crowded station.

"The trains run on 'Indian Standard Time,'" says Adnan with a sarcastic chuckle and a shrug, "and that means we could be here a while. If the train is delayed, there's nothing we can do but wait on the platform. Once one of my groups and I waited twelve hours on the platform! But hopefully we won't be delayed that long."

Even after all the affirmations and preparations, I feel my chest tighten and breaths shorten as my anxiety starts to take the reins. The platform is just a concrete slab with an overhang that provides some shade. There are no bathrooms anywhere. About a hundred feet down the track, a woman squats, relieving herself right on the rails. And I realize it's only a matter of time before that will be me. It's my only option.

This isn't uncommon in India. We haven't been in the country long, but I'd need two hands to count the number of people, men and women, that I've seen relieve themselves literally in the middle of the street.

Our group finds a place to sit and wait until our train decides to show up. I try to stay as still and cool as I can, breathing deeply and sipping on my water, while Tim wanders around the crowded platform, smiling his warm smile at locals who agree to let him take their picture.

I still haven't let him know how sick I am. He knows something's not right, but not the extent of it. Part of me hopes that if I don't make it real by speaking it, I can fend it off. Maybe I'm just one more bathroom break away from being done with it. How annoying would it be to tell him that I'm really sick only for it to resolve itself on the next bathroom trip?

When I'm sure he's not watching me, I crumple over my crossed legs, not caring that my face comes so close to the platform floor. I'll do anything to relieve this vice grip burning through my middle. Nothing helps. My clothes feel too tight. Hot flashes surge through my body only to leave in an icy wake as my sweat dries in the heat.

It's quite apparent now: I am not well, and I can't sit out here for twelve hours. Tim starts to pick up on my distress. He keeps asking me if I'm okay.

Less than fifteen minutes later, however, the ground starts to rumble, and Adnan readies the group. "This is ours!" I've never been so happy to see a train. Maybe I don't need to tell Tim after all. Maybe I can just find my seat, settle in, and let my body work through whatever is torturing it.

We fight our way through the crowd to board and find that a large family has settled into our seats. Adnan argues with them loudly in a language we don't understand. But they aren't moving. Adnan walks us away to a different compartment.

"The tour company buys extra seats in case this happens," he explains. We sit down next to an elderly, barefoot couple who are on their way to a wedding.

"Would you please consider giving me your seat?" implores the elderly man of me in eloquent but heavily accented English. "I am old and cannot climb well." Then he laughs loudly. I realize he's talking about tonight, when the seats around us fold down and become bunks. He wants my bottom bunk in exchange for his top bunk.

I trade with him, mostly to put an end to the conversation. I urgently need to find the bathroom. I think the trade annoys Adnan, who went through so much to get us the best bunks. But what Adnan doesn't know is that I'm from the southern United States, where ladies are raised not to ask for anything, even if we need it, lest we be a minor inconvenience. Bless our hearts. I don't know if my body will allow me to scale a ladder and climb into a top bunk, but in the words of regional icon Scarlett O'Hara, "I can't think about that now." Pushing it all to the back of my mind, I set off to find the bathroom.

It's at the far end of the next car. I have to step over the joint between train cars to get to it. It is technically a Western toilet, but there's no seat, no flushing, and, looking into the hole at the bottom of the grimy bowl, I can see the tracks whizzing by.

It's not perfect, but it's here, it's private, and I'm grateful.

The setting sun is painting the sky in indigos with streaks of pink. Solitary stars are beginning to pop through the smog. Even in my abdominally afflicted haze I can appreciate the striking scenery: trees and small buildings pepper the flat, sandy countryside. It stretches out in every direction to the feet of far-off mountains. People bike and walk alongside the train tracks. The soft, dreamy light quiets the naturally loud colors of their saris and turbans. The train window is like a watercolor painting.

There's a small jolt, and the entire train suddenly stops within a small cluster of buildings in the middle of the arid landscape. People crowd together to peer out the windows. Something is blocking the tracks.

Two hours creep sluggishly by, the sun disappearing to make way for the moon, and we're still at a standstill. After every trip back from the bathroom, I make my way back to our seats and find Tim's worried face scanning mine. "Are you sure you're okay?" I don't know, but I'm managing so far.

My fellow passengers mill about. Some make their way to doors at either end of the train car to buy *samosas* piled high on platters held aloft by enterprising locals looking to make easy rupees. The older man enjoying my former bunk pops the menthol-like hearts of cardamom pods into his mouth again and again and again.

I look out the windows to the train's left and right during another trip to the bathroom, and countless headlights glare back at me, streaming through the smudged plexiglass. Cars, tuk-tuks, and motorcycles are piling up on both sides of the tracks. Until the train moves, this little town is split in two.

Adnan shakes his head and stretches out in his seat. "The longer we sit here, the longer it will take to reach Agra." Obvious, but I hadn't put this together yet. Our original estimated trip time without delays was ten hours.

We're now looking at about thirteen hours of total trip time if there aren't any additional delays. Thirteen hours. And my stomach doesn't seem to be getting any better with each field trip to the bathroom. Eventually my body just empties completely. There's nothing left to purge, making each seizing cramp and wave of nausea torturous and unproductive.

In an attempt to stave off dehydration, I've blown through nearly all of my only liter of water with hours and hours to go before we reach Agra. Passengers on Indian trains like this one don't get drink service. There are no chipper attendants wheeling a cart down the aisle asking if anyone needs a soda or bag of peanuts. You bring your own fortifications, or you go without. On one of my many trips to the bathroom, I pass families whose mothers thoughtfully prepared elaborate meals, all packed neatly in stacking stainless steel lunch boxes. I only brought some protein bars and my water bottle.

"It's okay. I'm okay," I attempt to reassure myself on my millionth trip back from the bathroom. "I'm just going to go to bed, get some good sleep, and it'll make a world of difference. I just need to sleep it off."

At that very moment the train starts to move again. I let out an audible groan of relief that transcends language, judging by the faces of my fellow passengers. They nod in emphatic agreement.

Everyone slowly rouses themselves, and we begin working together to convert the train car benches into bunks. Stacked three high, one on top of the other, the bunks are wooden platforms topped with five-inch pleather-covered padding. They feel like the seats of your average diner booth. Downing the last of my water, I struggle up the ladder and into my traded top bunk. Unsurprisingly, I sleep poorly. Hardly at all, actually. The older man enjoying my assigned bottom bunk snores so loudly, I question whether or not he's pulling a prank on us.

The sun rises as we pull into Agra, and everyone starts collecting their things to disembark. The dehydration and lack of sleep have made my sickness worse (shocker). I have intense body aches, fever, chills, dizziness, and dilated eyes. I can't lift my bag. I can barely stand for more than a few minutes at a time. In the smoggy morning light, Tim realized just how sick I've become. Now he carries both our huge backpacks through the crowded station. He slows his pace so he can stay right next to me. "I'm sorry, baby," he murmurs.

I squint against the sun and try my best to keep walking while the city's eyes take in my leggings, and a thought pops into my head. An angry, indignant thought. A thought that has often frequented my mind since the Breaking:

I did not ask for this.

In fact, I did everything in my power to actively avoid this very situation. I declined street lassi and avoided menus-worth of regional delicacies. I washed and sanitized my hands religiously. I kept my mouth shut in the shower. I tried to put only steaming-hot food in my mouth, and yet here I am: sick out of my mind. And I'm not resentful, but, just for the record, the people in our group who have risked raw food or street lassi are all feeling fine.

I don't realize it immediately, but tears are streaming down my face. I'm not sad. I'm furious. And I'm completely exhausted by my total lack of control. In the months immediately after the Breaking I felt these same surges of anger. It often bubbled up in response to nothing in particular in a way that didn't make much sense. Sometimes I would have to remove myself from people, even Tim, confessing, "I'm sorry, I'm just really angry right now, and I'm not sure why." It was like my body, independent of my brain, would randomly remember the injustice of it all and surge into fight mode on my behalf.

Feeling angry on my own behalf is not something that I'm very comfortable with. I don't think many people are, especially women; it's much easier for us to get angry on behalf of someone else. If you hurt me, I can swallow my words, but if you hurt my friend or spouse or kid, I'm going to speak up.

So I stuffed my anger down deep where it could fester and grow like an unpopped blister. When I started working with my therapist, however, she encouraged me to give myself the space to be angry. She said things like, "You have a right to feel angry about what happened to you. You have a right to fume and rail about the way things should have gone. What happened was tragic, and you deserved better. You deserved so much better."

Before the Breaking I never thought twice about the phrase "in spite of," even though it includes a pretty barbed word: spite. But it makes sense because to thrive in spite of tragedy, you have to permit yourself to bring that spite. You have to sit with her barbs and her mess. And there *will* be a mess. Processing anger is like cleaning out your attic: it's going to get worse before it gets better.

There wasn't anyone my spite didn't target. It was a landmine that exploded with no regard to who was friend or who was foe. I was angry at Tim. I was angry at God. I was angry at myself for being too stupid to foresee the Breaking, as if anyone ever can. But, in the words of the unnamed poet, "I sat with my anger long enough, until she told me her real name was grief."

That's what this anger truly is: white-hot grief.

Grief for the life you would have lived, the story you should have had.

Grief for the pre-trauma version of yourself that no longer exists.

Grief for the lost belief that you have any control over the things that happen to you.

It wasn't until I grieved, really grieved, the passing of these things that I began to see the tigress and follow after her.

I collapse when we reach our hotel room. Tim and Adnan make a call, and two doctors come directly to the hotel. I don't know what wonder drugs they give me or what the pills are for, but I sleep for almost twenty-four hours.

When our alarm goes off the following morning, my stomach is miraculously calm. My muscles feel thin and shaky, and my head feels like something is boring its way out from the inside, but I'm not nauseous. I'm not running to the bathroom. I can deal with this.

I missed most of the Agra experiences while I slept, but thankfully the biggest experience was always planned for today: the Taj Mahal. Our group assembles, bleary-eyed but eager, in the front lobby at 4:00 AM and sets out for the entry gates of one the most popular tourist attractions in the world. It's so early that for once we're almost the only ones in line. Again we are asked to remove our shoes, or if we'd rather, they have elastic-rimmed cloth slips we can place over the soles of our shoes instead.

When we finally get our first look at that iconic white dome, the sun has just cleared the horizon. It burns through the heavy smog and bathes the grounds in a soft, hazy light. There's a long, expertly manicured mall between us and the base of the Taj: short, leafy trees, scrubby bushes, and pink blooming flowers dot the landscape. A shallow canal runs lengthwise through the mall, but it's currently dry. Sitting at its edge is the bench made famous when Princess Diana, in the depths of marital conflict, was photographed on it in 1992.

Slender-limbed monkeys scamper up trees and along railings as we listen to Adnan explain how the monument was commissioned by the Mughal Emperor Shah Jahan in 1632 as a mausoleum for his beloved wife, Mumtaz Mahal, who died in childbirth. The structure is completely symmetrical. The only nonsymmetrical element was added years after its completion: beside Mumtaz's sarcophagus is a second, slightly larger one, where the emperor himself was laid to rest.

This emperor, it's said, removed the tongues and hands of his chief architects after the completion of the project so that no other monument could rival it. Adnan insists that this is metaphor and that the emperor didn't literally maim people. In reality, he says, the leader rewarded his architects and artisans with so much wealth that they never needed to pursue work for the rest of their lives.

The turn of phrase used to describe this lavish retirement involves cutting off tongues and hands? I am beyond skeptical. I know too much about the darkest sides of people, particularly those with great power and wealth, to swallow this tourist-friendly take on the Taj's origin story.

There are four minarets that flank the great dome. These, Adnan explains, were intentionally built ever so slightly off kilter. It takes a minute to notice with the naked eye, but they lean outward so that, if they were to fall due to an earthquake or other cataclysmic event, they would fall away from the main structure.

Beyond the four minarets are two buildings that sit to the left and the right of the Taj: the Taj Mahal Mosque and the Jawab. These buildings are not white like the Taj and the minarets but a deep red sandstone. The contrast is striking. The mosque sits to the west of the Taj and faces Mecca, as all mosques should. The Jawab looks identical to the mosque, preserving the symmetry of the whole property, but because it doesn't face Mecca, it has always been used as an additional gathering space without the religious undertones.

The foundations of all these famous landmarks were constructed using, surprisingly, wood. They are comprised of timber from sal trees and an intricate system of wells that keep the wood wet (sal wood becomes stronger when it's wet). This spongy, shock-absorbing innovation was used to mitigate damage specifically in the event of an earthquake. It blows my mind to think that wood from trees that grew in the seventeenth century is holding all this up. It makes me feel so transient and fragile by comparison. How many disasters and wars and storms, how many Breakings, has this monument weathered?

Why am I struggling to weather just *one*?

Is it possible to build the equivalent safeguards into a person? Is there a way to be immune from the seismic chaos that comes with being a human? Can you install wood and wells into a psyche so that when the ground crumbles beneath a soul, they stand firm?

Then again, maybe we aren't supposed to be like mausoleums. They're solid, but they're also full of silence and death.

Maybe we, like stars, are born to collapse.

6
Midwives and Riptides

We load into a bus after our sunrise tour of the Taj and prepare to leave Agra. Our next destination is deep in the Rajasthani Desert: Tordi Garh. It's a small town south of Jaipur. Most tourists would never know it existed, but our tour company is invested in this community. They host clean-ups along the highways and have even raised money to install a beautiful soccer pitch for the local kids. In exchange, travelers like us are able to experience a more rural kind of Indian life. We just have to make it through a six-hour road trip first.

After an hour or two of driving, Adnan says something to the driver, who slows the bus and pulls off in front of a roadside stand. Adnan jumps out, and when he returns, his arms are loaded up with water bottles and blue drink cans.

"Would anyone care for a Thums Up?" he offers. "They are cold, but the water is not, unfortunately."

"What's a Thums Up?" Tim asks.

"It is Indian Coca-Cola." Adnan grins and hands me a cold can. On the front is a big red cartoon hand with its thumb up.

Thums Up truly is an Indian take on classic Coke. There's a little spiciness in the back of your throat when you drink it, not unlike the heat that comes with a sip of Mexican Hot Chocolate. Otherwise, it tastes just like that classic cola flavor. My eyes smart as the carbonation prickles my nose. Later I would look up the Thums Up backstory and learn that Coca-Cola stopped supplying to India in the 1970s because the government wanted them to disclose their secret formula. The huge hole they left in the market was filled by Thums Up, a competitive drink created by an Indian beverage company. Several decades later the Indian government relinquished some mandates, which made it possible for companies like Pepsi and Coca-Cola to sell in India again. But they could never beat Thums Up, who maintained eighty-five percent of the market share. Eventually Coca-Cola bought Thums Up. Which is a thumbs down. Still, I guess the little guy got quite the payday.

Close to noon we stop at a McDonald's, of all things. I'm still a bit peaky, so I refrain, but it's interesting to see the Indian version of the chain so well-known in the States. Little green dots next to menu items indicate which items are vegetarian-friendly. Red triangles indicate meat is used as an ingredient. Contrary to the McDonald's I'm familiar with, most of the menu caters to vegetarians. These "burger" patties are comprised of an assortment of mashed potatoes, peas, and spices molded into a patty shape and deep fried.

Before we get back on the road, we all hit the bathroom again. Another squatty potty. It's always a squatty potty when we're on the road. Somewhere along the way I got tired of having to clean my silicone funnel after every use, so this time I decide to try to use the facilities like a local. And, what do you know, I don't fall in!

It's a small win, but I'll take what I can get.

Driving through the country, even the rural areas, I realize that there is never a time I don't see throngs of people. There are over a billion people in India, and it shows: crowds standing outside shops, crowds walking beside the road, crowds on wheels filling the streets. Many times over the course of our trip I find myself struck by the fact that every single person I see is living a life as complex and rich and valid as mine. I try to take mental snapshots of people: a woman silhouetted in the doorway of a Nepalese building, a man standing at an outdoor pump splashing water on his face, two children playing with homemade kites.

They were here, walking around on our planet, for hundreds of days prior to my arrival, and they will go on—living their lives, fighting their battles, loving their people—long after I head back home. To many of them, I was just a face in the window of a passing bus. Most didn't even know I was there.

It was overwhelming to think about this. I heard the fragments of the person I was before my trauma, the Shiny-Happy-Brave Evangelist, chirp an idiom about the eternal destination of all these people. "We should feel an urgency to reach them!" she croaked, like a toy whose batteries were just about to give up the ghost.

In my youth I attended summer camps where we would do street evangelism. On Wednesdays, we would spend all afternoon "witnessing" to strangers on the street: asking them if they believed in heaven and hell, trying to engage them in conversation and hopefully conversion. I think back to the questions we were trained to ask and how triggered I would be if someone asked me those same questions now: "What happens when you die?" If their answer didn't line up with what Western Protestant Christianity teaches, we were to press, "How do you know?" We were also supposed to drill into their vocabulary with a "What do you mean by . . . ?" "What do you mean by purgatory?" "What do you mean by karma?" Followed by a truly callous "What if you're wrong?"

The mere fact that we were taught a sequence of questions that in no way gave real consideration to people's answers shows how misguided this training was, though I do have grace for the person I was. That eager little evangelist didn't know how deep the darkness of doubt could be. She had never laid in bed at 3:00 AM and felt unspeakable abandonment and emptiness. How could she have any empathy or understanding for others experiencing that?

To be fair, I don't know if this type of evangelism is fully right or wrong. The magician Penn Jillette is known for saying that if the story of Jesus is true, every Christian should devote every minute to this kind of balls-to-the-wall evangelism because that is the only appropriate response. I can understand this reasoning. But on the other hand, if I were to advocate for any type of evangelism—and at this point I'm not even sure that I would—I think it should more resemble the work of a midwife and less the work of a lawyer or a salesman. No more debating or strategizing or memorizing. More listening. More empathy. Less angling to make a quick sale, pray the magic words, and move on to the next unsuspecting stranger. More care. More patience to sit in the long hours of struggle as a new life begins.

I think it should involve "witnessing," but not as evangelicals define it. They think of witnessing the way the American justice system does: as the act of standing and reciting a practiced story to convince listeners. The result is a very "me-focused" performance that pushes listeners toward the speaker's desired outcome. Just like that camp script I recited at people. I think followers of Jesus should adopt the more "others-focused" definition: to witness is to watch, to see. We're not here to argue and convince. We're here to attend and be present.

While there are hours left before I meet the people of Tordi Gahr, outside my window the crowds buzz by in a never-ending stream of humanity. Everyone else on the bus is asleep, but I can't close my eyes. I can't look away. I can only offer the swarming masses, my fellow travelers, the briefest second of eye contact as they pass. A moment of attention. A moment of presence. A witness.

Before, on the Ganges, it had seemed so scary.

But now, suddenly, I feel starved for it.

Finally, we arrive. While we're here, we'll be staying in a fortress built in the eighteenth century. Descendants of the fort's founders have converted it to a bed and breakfast. It's a beautiful three-story, cream-colored building with deep red accents that almost look like they were dyed with henna. The building wraps like a horseshoe around a patio sprawled in the middle of the second floor. Doors to each of the suites line the perimeter of this shared outdoor space.

Just inside the turquoise-painted double doors, the receptionist, friendly and shy by turns, hands us our room key. It's a little skeleton key with a metal tag attached bearing the royal family's coat of arms and our room number: 406. Before we turn to gather our bags, the receptionist applies a red *bindi* between everyone's eyebrows with the tip of her ring finger. This is probably the most quintessential visual characteristic of someone from India or of a practicing Hindu, the dot between the eyebrows.

"What does it mean?" I ask her, curious to get an answer from a real person. Not from research, not from Google, but from someone who chooses to wear one every day.

"It is a blessing," she answers. And maybe it's the way she nods her head to me in a half wobble or the way her eyes wrinkle warmly with her smile, but I do feel like I've been blessed.

As a student, I was anointed not once but twice by an opprobrious televangelist at the private college he founded. This happened because I was present at two different campus-wide convocations where he and some other faculty anointed the student body. Somehow I was funneled toward him both times. His palsied hands were supposed to make a cross on my forehead with some type of special oil. It ended up more closely resembling the figure of a jellyfish and made my skin break out.

I much prefer the bindi.

Tim and I shlep our bags up winding stairs to the third floor and catch our breath while enjoying the view of the little village. It's not long before we're called to the large dining room on the second floor for dinner. It's the first full meal I've dared to eat since my stomach tried to kill me, and I cautiously enjoy measured bites as the sun sinks below the sand dunes.

The village cultivates its own produce, dairy, and poultry. It's a difference you can taste in the authentic, homemade Indian dinner we're served: chicken biryani, a mild creamy green soup (that I request a second bowl of), and fresh roti with chutney for dipping. I also ask for a chai because I'm quickly becoming an addict.

In the morning after breakfast, three women from the village come to the fort and make one of my tourist dreams come true: they apply bewitching, swirling henna to my hands. Even Tim gets in on it and asks for one of the henna artists to write "India" in Hindi on his forearm. Afterward we get ready to tour the village on foot.

Hidden down a side street, a rustle of brightly colored fabrics catches our attention. A small group gathers near the entrance to a home, kids and women all dressed in colorful saris. They sing, clap, and chat together. A small boom box blares from somewhere. The women are so beautiful in their easy realness wrapped in bright, silky rainbows. The American monochromatic, farmhouse aesthetic has drained vivid colors like these from my day-to-day life, but they are India's normal.

When the women notice our group spying, they smile warmly and wave. The kids wade through the pool of saris to run over to us. Before we know it, we're being pulled in. The children and most of the women are having a great time teaching our group how to do Bollywood dance moves and asking for selfies. I watch, holding back a bit near Adnan.

"They are getting ready for a wedding," he explains. "It will probably happen in the next few weeks. They are celebrating the bride."

One woman wrapped in a sari of gold and deep red is making her way through the small crowd to each member of our group. When she gets to me, she ties a thin red and gold twine around my wrist. With a smile and a friendly head wobble, she rejoins the dancing.

"That's the bride," says Adnan, "and that means you've been invited."

There's a very distinct feeling of isolation that haunts trauma survivors. Whether it's little t trauma (the kind that can come from just being a human in the world today) or big T Trauma, the recovery process can feel pretty lonely. Along with the big T or little t comes incredible nuance because, of course, your trauma story is layered, complicated, and absolutely unique—and this on top of whatever baseline betrayal, loss, or grief you're dealing with. These latter archetypal trauma themes are riptides that threaten to pull you under while the nuanced details of your unique story are waves that crash unrelenting, one after the other, into your face.

Because none of my friends and family knew or understood the complexity of my "waves," I felt very isolated. I mistakenly believed that to be fully seen and supported, I needed every one of my waves to be known. My therapist knew them all, of course, and my interactions with her were unspeakably healing. So I tried to find that same level of solace in other relationships, assuming that I just needed to be as forthcoming with them as I was with her. But there is a difference between being seen and being supported. They aren't mutually exclusive, but they're also not the same.

If I step into the shoes of my friends and family members, I will admit that being the recipient of an unexpected "trauma dump" is scary. It can trigger our own feelings of anxiety, fear, or anger. We might start projecting, fumbling our way through advice that has more to do with us than you, or we might tell you one of our own personal stories that only peripherally ties into what you're going through. Because this is the only way we know how to relate.

We might be overcome with feelings of failure or incompetence because we wonder, *How could we not have known?*

We might be alarmed at the dark humor you've adopted just to get through the day.

We might panic, feeling like it's suddenly our responsibility to help you fix your situation. Because we love you.

All of this because we love you, even if all these responses have more to do with calming the sudden storm within us than in truly helping you.

The truth is that no one in this emotional state is fit to shepherd your healing. None of us are at our best when we're triggered. I get that now. Mental health professionals are trained to help us heal. Spouses are not. Friends and family are not. Most religious leaders and church staff are not. Strangers on the internet, as a whole, are not.

I hope this is obvious to you because it wasn't to me, and that's what led me to open up to a handful of people. I thought for them to support me, they needed to know every gnarly detail. Every wretched fact. But I'm realizing now that this was an illusion. The sharing of every detail of our tragedies will not, in itself, cure our isolation. In some ways over-sharing can actually hinder connectedness and intimacy. Even if they know every detail, people will still very rarely understand the length and breadth of your suffering, and their inability to comprehend, even after you've laid bare your blistered soul, can be extremely hurtful and only amplify that isolation.

This is what happened to me. It's what caused me to turn inward, to avoid eye contact. To master the "Fine, how are you?" But this withdrawal didn't fix the problem; it still left me isolated.

So maybe an in-between is possible. Because we do need people, which was a difficult thing for me to accept after suffering such a massive loss of trust with my own Breaking followed by these smaller everyday betrayals.

I wish I could say that healing is possible in a vacuum, but that's just not the case. Having an inner circle of trusted, safe voices to speak into your healing and know every one of your waves is critical. Most people, even if they mean well, won't be up to the task, so choose this circle carefully. Maybe it's also possible to create an outer network of support from people that understand our suffering on a different level. A riptide level.

Grief, loss, and betrayal have swept many out to the sea of trauma before us, and many will come after. We think we're completely alone initially because our waves threaten to overwhelm us, but it's not true. There are so many people to the left and right of us. Sure, your waves are different from theirs. But we're all in the same riptide, fighting the same undertow. This is another reason why I decided not to fill these pages with the specifics of my unique Breaking; I didn't want to tell you a story about my waves. I wanted to come alongside you—the ones in my same riptide—and let you know you're not alone out here.

These were the most soothing moments in my own recovery, when my isolation began to melt away: the moments when I found people swirling in my same riptide. They didn't know all the gory details of my Breaking, and I didn't know theirs. But they also didn't shout magic-bullet hacks to beat the riptide from the safety of shore, like my other friends and family. They just simply said, "This sucks. I get it. I feel the same way. You're not alone."

Like a little red and gold twine tied around my wrist, this camaraderie between sufferers was not much. But just like the beautiful gesture by the bride during our visit in Tordi Garh, it was enough to let me know I was invited, a part, included, remembered, seen, and supported. It was enough to send my isolation running and give me the strength to keep my head lifted and eyes on the shore.

7
A Special Kind of Stuck

A few hours on a bus lands us in Jaipur. We're only here for one day, so we make a beeline to the Amer Fort as soon as we drop our bags at the hotel. We're starting to get the hang of this whole tourist-in-India thing, although after being treated like celebrities in Tordi Garh, many in our group (including me, if I'm honest) feel a little snobby to be suddenly surrounded by other tourists again. They're everywhere, especially at the fort.

Sitting proud atop a barren, clay-colored hill, the Amer Fort is about four hundred years old and looks like it was carved out of the very earth. Built by Raja Man Singh I in 1592, its strategic hilltop location made it a strong military base and impressive royal residence for Rajput rulers. Steep cobbled walkways with hairpin turns crisscross up the hillside to the mouth of the fort's entrance. You can either hoof it yourself, or you can catch a ride on a brightly painted elephant. Most tourists opt for the later. But Adnan tells us about the abhorrent treatment and living conditions these creatures endure and encourages us not to support it with our cash.

It's hard to make eye contact with one of these animals, standing just a few feet away, and not feel profoundly moved. We unanimously agree to make the hike together. It's a relatively easy trek and we're rewarded with an up-close look at spacious garden courtyards, elaborate mirrored mosaics, and a stunning fusion of Rajput and Mughal architecture.

After the fort we ramble through Jaipur's famous street markets. Vendors display their wares on rolling carts, on blankets stretched over the cracked pavement, and hanging off their bodies. They shout and wave at us to consider their goods. We walk by a *spicewallah's* stall, and the air is so heavy with chili powder, coriander, and saffron that most people in our group start coughing. A relentless man selling small drums follows us, thrumming and tapping, until I cave and buy one for my brother.

We enjoy piping hot street chai and take selfies with locals. Later we catch a Bollywood film (*Baaghi 2*) in the huge Raj Mandir Cinema, a place full of what looks like attempted opulence on the tightest of budgets. In the lobby several large art deco chandeliers give off a bright, almost blue-tinted light while symmetrical stairs curve in a horseshoe shape around the perimeter and rise to the balcony entrance doors. The massive pink interior looks more like the stage theaters I'm familiar with than a cinema. In the States, our movie theaters are steep; the seats are tiered so that our feet are almost level to the head of the person seated in front of us. Not so in this theater. The pitch of the floor is more gradual and the number of seats far greater than any I've seen in a regular stateside cinema.

We take our seats on the ground floor, the lights dim, and I gain a love for Bollywood almost immediately. It's an easy jump since I already love musicals, and it's made even better by the fact that movie theater audiences in India are more enthusiastic than the audiences I've seen in America: dancing in the aisles during the dance scenes, shouting at the characters on screen, cheering. Tim likes to be the first to clap, rallying a wave of applause mostly for the heck of it. He doesn't speak Hindi, but he gets his cues from the intensity of the dialogue and the swell of the soundtrack, and our fellow audience members are more than happy to join in when he starts.

It's a blast, and afterward Adnan confirms we didn't experience anything out of the ordinary. That's just how India goes to the movies.

Before dinner with our group, Tim and I decide to hunt down some gifts for people back home. We planned to wait until the end of our trip to souvenir shop because we didn't want to carry around a heap of added stuff across India. Now, with only one more city to visit, we're ready to load up.

We walk a short distance to a grocery store where we won't need to haggle over every transaction and decide to keep it simple by getting everyone a taste of our favorite Indian experience: loose-leaf chai tea. We can sense fellow shoppers' eyes on us as we walk through aisles of packaged snacks and bottled drinks, but it doesn't feel so strange now, not nearly as scary as it did in Varanasi. A trio of young siblings even runs up to us, grabbing our hands and begging for selfies, and I acquiesce as easily as if they were my nieces and nephews.

It feels regrettable to finally be this comfortable in India the evening before our last stop.

The next morning we leave early for Delhi. When I ask Adnan the best way to mail a postcard, he reacts like I asked him to swallow the bus, wincing and shaking his head. Unbeknownst to me, India's mail is less than reliable, especially when it comes to international addresses. Perhaps as a way to placate me, he suggests I pay the bellhop manning the hotel lobby desk to mail it for me. He tells me he's certain the kid will pocket my cash and just trash the card, but if he does decide to help, it might work. I have to try.

It's a tradition I started some time ago: I mail my wanderlustful husband a postcard during big trips. Usually when we get home, there's a little piece of wherever-we-were waiting in the mailbox. We've got a little stack of messages sent from South Africa, Loch Ness, Edinburgh, Isle of Skye, Piccadilly Circus, Kona, and Cannes. I would love to add a pretty Taj Mahal postcard to the pile, but I have to pin that hope to the heart of a stranger as we pile into the bus.

We take a train into the nation's capital. It's sleek, more modern than the overnight train, with airplane-esque seats and big windows on either side. As it hurdles toward Delhi, our last stop after thirteen days of traveling, I feel my old life pulling me back. I can't wait to see my dog and my family again, and after pushing myself to be present and courageous during this trip, I feel less intimidated by my recovery process on the whole. If I can stare down panic in Kathmandu, I can definitely do it in my own home.

But I also feel a pit growing in my stomach. My dead-end job—the one that brings out the toxic in me—looms over what would be a sweet homecoming.

Several years prior to this trip, before the Breaking, I wrestled with this same feeling as another trip drew to a close. In a packed, low-roofed restaurant on a rainy night on the Isle of Skye, Tim asked me what I wanted to do differently once we got home. For him, there's nothing like an extended trip to put your life and routine in perspective. You gain fresh insight both on the things that you value (because you're probably missing them) and the things that are weighing you down (because you're not looking forward to returning to them). For Tim, New Year's

Eve is for tourists. The best time to make resolutions and goals is after a trip. So, over split pea soup with thick slices of toasted wheat bread, charcuterie, baked pears, and Skye Gold Ale, we made resolutions.

Tim already knew I was unhappy in my then relatively new job. But after spending that week with our tour guide—Jodie, a charismatic, exceedingly bright person who had clearly found a job she was uniquely and perfectly suited for—my own professional journey seemed especially grim. Jodie had exuded an effortless confidence. She was warm. She genuinely enjoyed her job. Jodie at work was diametrically different from me at work, and the chasm between the two created such an ache in me, I couldn't help but get choked up in that little wooden booth.

Now, years later while wrapping up this trip to India, nothing has changed. Same job. Same problems. Over the time since Skye I've submitted so many job applications, and I only have a folder of "We regret to inform you…" emails to show for it.

I'm trapped. And I'm not, in any way, the professional I hoped I'd be.

I know Tim is going to ask his end-of-trip questions when we get to Delhi. It feels like a special kind of stuck to give him the same answers I gave him all those years ago in Skye. But there's no fixing that right now, so I push it to the back of my mind as we rush on to our destination.

8
Seven Chilis and a Lime

Delhi is split into two: Old Delhi and New Delhi, the ancient and the modern cohabitating. The Qutb Minar, for example, is a 238-foot-tall minaret built around 1200 CE. It still stands in Delhi just a few miles from where jumbo jets take off and return from international destinations.

We all check into the hotel and then head out to see as much as possible. Rickshaws drop us off at an entrance of the Delhi metro, and Adnan huddles us into a circle to explain how this will work: men and women ride in separate trains here, so Tim and Adnan will take the men's train. The rest of us will have to make our way to the women's platform, board the women's train (one covered in totally-not-condescending pink, clip-art flower graphics), and then make sure we get off at the right stop.

It's no problem; we nail it like locals.

First stop is the Jama Masjid: a huge stone mosque, red as chili powder and crowned with three huge domes. Ornamental white designs, orderly and symmetrical, cover the walls. It reminds me of frosted gingerbread at Christmastime. I would read later that it was built in the middle of the seventeenth century, and it's one of the largest mosques in India. Our group pads up the steep stairs leading to the east gate where we leave our shoes and are given baggy, floor-length tunics to wear over our Western clothes. Walking through the towering stone archway into the expansive courtyard, I see devoted worshipers and tourists alike milling about. The covered alcoves that line the perimeter offer some shade and a dry, friendly draft, if you stand in the right place. And all around, men pray facing Mecca.

Everyone has a group of people they feel a special affinity for, I think. Maybe a certain nationality or religion. Or maybe not. Maybe seeing these distinctions is an American Christianity quirk I picked up at some vacation Bible school and still maintain. Either way, I have a special place in my heart for the followers of Allah. In the words of Yann Martel, "I challenge anyone to understand Islam, its spirit, and not to love it. It is a beautiful religion of brotherhood and devotion." I'm moved to tears as we walk into the beautiful inner courtyard of the mosque. On either side the faithful bow under cavernous, vaulted halls. Their prayers rise with the heat beneath the red stone arches.

My conception of prayer fractured after the Breaking, along with so many other things. Prayer was pitched to me as a secret weapon. A first and last resort. "Pray without ceasing," we're told. But what do you do when your prayers dissolve on your tongue?

Something prickly lodges itself in my chest whenever someone tells me to pray. "Just pray," they'll text, along with a prayer request for mundane, fleeting things, and I hate it. I know this isn't fair. Their prayer requests have nothing to do with me. But it irritates my healing soul to see someone spend the same number of breaths on a prayer about nothing that I spent on prayers for my everything.

My idea of prayer was permanently altered. Now I wonder if the devoted around me ever feel that way—like they're just going through the motions. Dipping a bucket into an empty well over and over and over again. Always coming up dry, yet always hoping that the next time will be different. The next time will justify it all.

Still, their devotion moves me. There's something to be said for the ones that show up anyway. Maybe I'm moved because I know that's not me. Maybe I'm moved because I know that could always change. I could still choose to be the one who shows up.

Leaving the mosque, we wind through crowded street bazaars toward Gurudwara Sis Ganj Sahib, a Sikh temple in Old Delhi. It should go without saying at this point but, of course, we stop for street chai. This chaiwallah is tucked behind the bustle of the street in a little side alley, high wires as thick as my forearm sagging above his stall. A long-legged, white street dog with black spots dozes nearby in the shade of a doorstop. Decorating the various ledges and lips jutting out of the alley wall are tiny, brightly colored figurines of Shiva and Ganesha. And hanging near them is an ornament I've seen all over India's shops and vehicles: seven chilis stacked broadsides together on top of a small lime, all strung together to form a little tassel.

"What is that?" I ask Adnan.

"Seven chilis and a lime," he replies, as if it's obvious.

"What does it mean?"

"It's like . . . a good luck," he says, with a sip of chai in between. Later I would look up the origin of this good luck charm and find a few different explanations. The most superstitious theory is that people leave these ornaments for the goddess of misfortune, Alakshmi. She purportedly snacks on them, appeased by her favorites, and takes her misfortune elsewhere. Some people suggest that the smell of these dangles works as an old-world insecticide and helps to repel mosquitoes and biting insects. Others suggest that travelers used to attach these tassels to their saddles and carts. The lime (or sometimes a lemon) was added to drinking water to help quench travelers' thirst along the way. And in the event they were bitten by a snake or insect, they could bite into a chili. If they couldn't taste the heat, that meant their nervous system was failing and that the offending critter was venomous.

Regardless of which explanation is truly behind this tradition, it's fun to see it persisting in the modern world. We can trick ourselves into believing we're profoundly modern, evolved beyond the shackles of superstition, but then we discover that we're not that far removed from our predecessors after all, thanks to little reminders like a dangling stack of chilis atop a lime.

As our group heads toward the temple, I realize the only meager thing I know about Sikhism is what Adnan tells us during our fifteen-minute walk. We can't wear our shoes, we'll have to wash our feet before entering, and we'll need to wear a head covering. The brick sidewalk in front of the temple has a trough about a foot wide running the length of the front entrance cradling a shallow stream of clear water. We remove our shoes and step into the stream to wash our feet.

Once we're clean, we enter a small room just off of the main sanctuary. We'll leave our shoes here with dozens of others. Rhythmic melodies carried on a crowd's voice seep through the walls. This is where non-Sikh visitors receive their head covering before entering the sacred building. It's a simple handkerchief. I tie the corners into a knot at the nape of my neck as we enter the sanctuary through a side door.

The room is richly colored and expansive. Columns that meet in scalloped arches support a second-story balcony that wraps around the perimeter. At the front sits a brilliant gold structure atop a stage. The structure itself is pagoda-shaped and resting proudly under a red cloth suspended from wires attached to the balcony. Two musicians and a singer lead the congregants in a hymn from the left-hand side of the stage.

The congregants themselves are dressed almost exclusively in white: the men with their regal mustaches and beards and pleated turbans, the women with their flowing saris and scarves. They sit cross-legged on the carpeted floor or stand close to the stage, singing and clapping in time with the music. We find a spot near the back of the room and take a seat. A TV attached to the underside of the balcony displays the lyrics to the worship song in Hindi and English. They are generic in their praise and remind me so much of the formulaic songs sung in every evangelical church back home: we praise you, we thank you, etc.

The song ends, and Adnan beckons us on through the sanctuary, past the stage and musicians, under another arch. He points out notable architecture as we meander through hallways, our bare feet whispering softly on the cold stone floors, until we reach the kitchens and the true worship.

Filling a labyrinth of rooms are dozens and dozens of Sikhs, cooking. Still more Sikhs buzz between these rooms carrying dirty dishes to be washed or clean dishes ready to be used by the one hundred or so diners waiting in the cavernous dining hall. This is a *langar*: a communal meal. Sikhs come to these kitchens and cook around the clock, Adnan tells us. Twenty-four hours a day, 365 days a year, this Sikh community cooks for anyone who happens to need a meal. No one is turned away. Incredibly, in this temple alone they feed over thirty-five thousand people on an average day, as many as a hundred thousand on holidays. And every meal is free.

Close to twenty people anointed in flour sit cross-legged around a low table rolling fist-sized balls of dough into flat chapatis. More people in the next room take the doughy disks and brush them with a generous helping of ghee (clarified butter) before they frisbee the flat dough onto table-sized grills. As the dough fluffs and browns, still more workers flip the flatbreads. They have to stretch over the expansive grill with four-foot-long iron spatulas to reach them all.

In another room men stand like gondoliers around huge brass woks large enough to cook over twenty-five hundred pounds of food at one time. Men stir steaming vegetable curries, lentil dahl, and mountains of rice with ladles attached to handles that are as long as the men are tall. Their *karas*, the simple bracelet worn by all Sikhs to signify their commitment to God, catch the afternoon light as they heave the steamy, fragrant masses.

I don't remember my first communion—participating in it for the first time isn't as big a deal in evangelical churches as it is in other traditions. I do, however, remember my fascination with the little cups as a young child, how the tasteless rectangle wafers looked like tiny Poptarts and got stuck in my molars. And I remember communion being very rare, a stiff and somber thing that happened seemingly only a few times a year. The pastor would stand and speak the words Jesus spoke during his last meal: "This is my body, broken for you . . . This is my blood . . . Do this in remembrance of me."

Later as an adult (but before the Breaking), I heard a sermon that completely transformed my expectations and understanding of this ritual. In a warehouse church in Atlanta, a pastor posited that when Jesus spoke the words above, maybe he wasn't asking that his followers eat a holy cracker very seriously every so often in church. Do this in remembrance of me? Maybe the "this" he was referencing was what he and his followers were doing at the moment he said those words: sitting together and sharing a meal. Not meditating together on Jesus's sacrifice (which, of course, had not happened yet) but simply enjoying a meal together.

Nothing more or less than langar.

That scorching afternoon in a Sikh temple, I feel like I am seeing one of the most unadulterated examples of communion. People of all backgrounds and faiths eating together. Because that's the one thing about Jesus's table that is undeniable: everyone was welcome. While the religious safeguarded their spaces and found pride in those with whom they refused to break bread, Jesus was the opposite. He ate with shunned tax collectors, unclean sinners, wild zealots, and women called promiscuous.

I could have stayed in those kitchens until the sun threw long shadows across the floured hands and full plates, but the road home is calling. As we collect our shoes, a part of me aches to feel the purpose and camaraderie that I imagine this Sikh community feels as they feed the masses. At this point in the story, I'm not sure if that exists outside of a religious institution.

Here is where our tour comes to an end. Our last group dinner is at a big table in the outdoor courtyard of a restaurant. The dusty Delhi sunset rims everything in gold. We order sweet lime sodas and paneer and rotis and all the things we've learned to love during our trip. We treat Adnan to a glass of whiskey as a token of our appreciation. And as we're all leaning back in our chairs, lips loosened by alcohol and good food and nearly two weeks of time spent together, our group starts to talk about religion. It's been a huge part of our trip, after all. We've explored mosques and temples and shrines together. We attended ceremonies and observed rituals side by side. I'm honestly surprised we haven't discussed it until now.

Most of the people at the table are agnostic or atheist. Adnan says that he is a Protestant. His specificity is a little surprising to me, but then again, the term isn't one I hear a lot in my day-to-day life. My Catholic friends as well as my Protestant friends both tend to use the general term *Christian* to describe themselves.

When everyone's eyes turn to me, I hesitate. Looking back, I would see this as a bit of a watershed moment, but right now, with my head sorting through all the complicated tangles woven around my perception of spirituality and God and trauma and recovery, it feels right to tell it to them this way:

"I'm a Jesus person."

Because, even against the backdrop of everything, I have to be honest with myself and admit I can't get over the Red Letters. I can't help but be drawn to that woodworking storyteller who upset the religious establishment and called them out on their bullshit. Who was more likely to be found eating at the table than praying at the temple. Who advocated peace over vengeance and love over judgment. Who sought out the people everyone else thought were unlovable or weird or dirty and said, "You're my kind of people."

Who just showed up and was present with us.

There's a moment in the book *Life of Pi* when Pi first encounters Jesus, this "troublesome rabbi of long ago," in a conversation with a priest he meets at a small church in the hills of Munnar, India. Initially, Pi is full of disbelief and annoyance: Here is Christianity's single god (there's only one, unlike in Pi's Hinduism, which has hundreds), and he gets hungry, thirsty, tired and sad and anxious. He's heckled and harassed. His followers misunderstand him, and his opponents disrespect him. "What kind of god is that?" Pi wonders. "It's a god on too human a scale, that's what." He is unimpressed with Jesus's miracles, which are also on a very human scale: eyes are healed, bellies are filled, water is momentarily walked on. "Any Hindu god can do a hundred times better," asserts Pi.

What else did this god-man do while on earth? Pi is baffled to learn that most of his life was spent telling stories, and when Jesus wasn't talking, he was traveling, mostly on foot, in a hot place under the thumb of Rome's oppression. "When he splurged on transportation," Pi complains, "it was a regular donkey. This Son is a god who died in three hours, with moans, gasps, and laments. What kind of god is that? What is there to inspire this Son?"

The priest listening to Pi simply replies, "Love." That's what ultimately compels Pi to the person of Jesus: his humanity and his love for the rest of humanity.

I realize on our last night in Delhi that I feel the same way. I love this man. And I think what he says and does is important. Beyond that, the jury's out. But suddenly I feel okay with that.

I don't have to figure it all out right now. I'm a Jesus person, and that's enough for me.

Before Tim and I make our way to the airport, a family connection has invited us to attend an event for visually-challenged Christians living in Delhi. They've asked if maybe I can snap a few photos with my professional-grade camera for the ministry to use. That's where Tim and I are headed now. I can feel myself bristling at the thought of going back into the world of the church, but it'll just take a couple of hours. So with thanks and hugs conveyed to our little group of traveling friends, we direct our rickshaw out of the hotel courtyard and away.

We pull up to a big office building and follow banners to a small hall with a modest stage at the front. I scout out where I can take the best photos without being distracting to the attendees. Before long the room is full of locals, and the program begins. This event is being held by a company that creates audio Bible devices with easy-to-navigate buttons.

They allow people who are visually challenged, non-literate, or part of an oral culture to independently engage in scripture.

Local speakers take turns at the podium, speaking some in English, some in what I guess to be Hindi. At the end of the presentations, three local believers, all visually challenged, are gifted their own audio Bibles. As soon as they find the right button on their devices, the Bible in their mother tongue begins to play, and their mouths fall open in incredulous smiles.

Behind the viewfinder of my camera, I feel my skin erupt into chill bumps. The recipients aren't mirroring the smile of someone around them. They aren't amping their expressions for the camera. I get the sense that had the source material been different, say *suras* from the Quran or the Hindu Vedas, the impact on the listeners' faces would have been the same. They are completely authentic in their joy at hearing words they hold sacred.

This moment feels weighty and real. This feels important.

Tim and I catch a ride to the airport. Our flight departs at 2:00 AM, so to kill time after passing through customs, I edit photos of believers accessing their holy scriptures independently for the first time.

I feel the tigress stir. There's so much waiting for me on the other side of this flight: A dead-end job. An ongoing struggle against my depression and anxiety. A fight for the recovery of myself and maybe my faith. It feels like I'm staring down an impossible assignment.

But as our wheels lift off the runway and I look down on the infinitely sprawling Delhi—a city that's been destroyed and rebuilt fifteen times—I think that maybe it's not impossible to rebuild a single life.

9
The Scariest Choice

It takes more than twenty-five hours to travel back. I read *Life of Pi* cover to cover, watch several movies, and still it feels like I have an eternity to wait in my plane seat. But finally, gloriously, we are home.

Home. The whole time I was away, I imagined home waiting for me exactly as she was when I left. And in many ways, she is. But as I settle back into my life, I can feel that things have changed. I changed.

Tim and I attempt to make chole and *aloo paratha*, a flatbread made with steamed potatoes and herbs. At one of our hotels I watched a young woman named Mini in the kitchen making aloo paratha and effortlessly moving between rolling out dough, tossing it onto the hot griddle, and pulling the perfectly toasted discs off just in time. She ended up scribbling her recipe down for me, but it's not the same when it's made in my kitchen.

I get clean water and a mountain of ice out of my fridge door like a queen. I enjoy the brief week of effortless early mornings before my body adjusts back to my home time zone. I sip my daily coffee made just the way I like it. It's luxurious, but I can feel my mind pacing. The audio Bible company, the one that hosted the event in Delhi, has made me a job offer. It happened not long after I got home.

The marketing manager would like more images and videos similar to the pictures I captured of real people using their product. Seeing my resume, which was full of other marketing skills and experiences, confirmed their interest. The position was entirely remote, they said, but it *would* require frequent trips to India.

And I'm conflicted. I don't know what the tigress would (or should) do.

This could very likely be a bad decision. Yes, it would get me out of my current toxic job, but I would take a pay cut. And because of our family connection to the company, I would need to submit my candidacy to the board of directors. No pressure.

I also remember the uncertainty of the flight into Nepal, the panic of that first night in Kathmandu. Could I do all that again? Multiple times a year? With the added weight of professional performance expectations once I'm on the ground?

The best advice for trauma survivors is not to rush your recovery. Trauma is weird and layered and often not immediately logical. It's very common to miss peripheral damage until weeks, months, or even years have passed, and then suddenly you're struggling with something that feels like a random problem, like nightmares or memory loss or hoarding, but it isn't. In reality, it's a delayed trauma response manifesting itself.

Would I be rushing my recovery if I took a position that required too much of me too soon? Even more important to consider, jumping into another conservative Christian community (one I would have to converse and collaborate with daily) would very likely chafe and irritate my bruised soul as most Christian circles had since the Breaking. Maybe it's too much, too soon.

Or maybe it's not.

Yes, the first twenty-four hours in Nepal were terrifying, as were the anger and sickness I experienced for different reasons in Agra. But I *survived* all of that. When it comes to fighting the shroud of depression and resisting the whispers of anxiety, my record is perfect. I survived every moment. I've won every battle. And I'm not the same girl who white-knuckled her way into the Himalayas.

It's very true that my relationship with the church and Christian people is complicated. I am navigating a personal recovery that feels like it's moving me away from evangelical Christianity. But taking this new job would allow me to help other people (people who might never have the opportunity) to independently experience those same Red Letters that somehow always surprise and comfort me. It feels worthwhile in a way that work hasn't for a long time.

I also never want it to be said of me that my opinions or thoughts or personal traumas prevented me from stepping into the ring. So I don't agree with most American evangelical Christian convictions? That's valid. But it gets harmful when I become so dogmatic about my beliefs that I stay in my own echo chamber, refusing to show up and attempt to live out a kinder, more thoughtful way. That is in fact a defining trait of ultra-religious people that I find appalling. And even though the opinions I hold are different from theirs, I'd be hypocritical if I allowed my views to keep me from getting my hands dirty. Why would I turn down an opportunity to do truly good work just because I sometimes don't agree with the people I'd be working with?

My brain ties itself in knots chasing pros and cons, and there's no sign of tiger stripes anywhere. After talking it to death with Tim, my therapist, and trusted friends, it's time for me to make a decision.

I quiet my mind, and finally, I hear the bold tigress, that reckless voice, rumble. "What, after all, would be the scariest choice?"

It's obvious, but nonetheless terrifying. So many beautiful, profound things happened during those two weeks in Nepal and India—and almost none of it was in my control. The only thing I could control was whether or not I continued to show up.

Healing and spirituality are both journeys. I realize I don't need to have everything figured out right now. I don't need to have all the answers. I just have to show up and follow the tigress. Even through the panic of Kathmandu and the suffering of Lumbini and the anger of Agra. I just have to keep showing up.

And that's what I decide to do.

A smattering of summer months pass, and I work to get acclimated to my new day job. As I suspected, the team is made mostly of conservative, highly committed religious people. But from the desk in my home office I'm able to keep that world mostly at arm's length and protect my raw heart. Mostly.

There are still moments that chafe: They pray before meetings. Several teammates speak in a way that assumes everyone around them agrees with their (usually quite conservative) opinions, and they can be derisive about contradicting perspectives. Not that any are ever really spoken.

Those bigger things are surprisingly easier for me to move past. Everyone's entitled to their own opinion, and I find I don't mind leaving them to theirs. It's the little things, the subversive things that threaten to impact my work in a way that upends my own philosophy, that are harder to swallow. For example, one of the things some of my new teammates (and other Christians in my circle) say when they hear I've been to

India is, "I'm sure you can just *feel the darkness* in a place like that." And every time someone says this to me, I think about . . .

The feeling of being seen by two bold women in the back of a boat on the Ganges.

The feeling of inclusion as a bride tied a red and gold twine around my wrist in Tordi Garh.

The feeling of being moved to tears while watching the fervent faces of the faithful in prayer at the Jama Masjid Mosque in Delhi.

I think about the Sikh's langar, and I think about the shy receptionist who daubed a bindi on my forehead in blessing, and I think about the barefoot man who traded bunks with me on a train, and I think about Adnan.

And then I try and fail to find the words to articulate to my new colleagues that "darkness" is the furthest thing from anything I ever felt in India.

The word is indicative of a worldview that observes a hierarchy when it comes to countries and people. Interestingly, I've never heard this sentiment expressed after someone's visited Paris or the Napa Valley. It's almost always reserved for places like Haiti, or China, or African countries, with a special exception made for the most liberal American cities like Hollywood and New York City. If a place is so dark that you can *feel* it, it's going to rank pretty low on the list. And just in case you're not up on your Christianese, this palpable darkness can be equated to sin, evil, wickedness, oppression, doom, or really anything that contradicts Christianity, including a different religion. Sometimes, because of the sinister smear-and-blur that is Christian Nationalism, it can also encompass anything that contradicts a politically conservative American worldview. And because the audio Bible ministry—now my ministry— is doing work in these "dark" nations populated by ethnically diverse people groups, my fear is that this hierarchical mentality will slouch into white saviorism.

Our team is predominately white and predominately male, from a fully industrialized nation, well-educated and wealthy—and we show up to spiritually "save" people. These attributes are so ubiquitous in my religious culture that I could be describing almost any American ministry, church staff, or outreach team. Part of me wonders if the white saviorism mentality is just an occupational hazard. Maybe it's even inevitable.

To be clear: I don't think any of the people who asked me if I could "feel the darkness" in India were intentionally hateful or smug. Many of them are kind people with good intentions. It's just one of those small, unexamined things Christians say that is indicative of a deeper problem. And it has a huge potential to harm.

I once heard a man who was born and raised in India talk about leading a group of missionaries through his home country. They said things in line with this sentiment, and even though he was a Christian himself and deeply invested in the work happening during these mission trips, it was very damaging for him.

How would you feel if someone said this about the place you call home?

As a member of the marketing team, I find myself sometimes fielding suggestions and requests from teammates for campaigns that are rooted in this hierarchical mentality. That's when things are hardest. That's when I feel like I'm suffocating a little bit. I quickly realize I'm going to have to be the one to filter out these and other outdated, harmful sentiments, and it feels overwhelming. How can I, as a newly hired young woman at the bottom of the org chart, explain this to a male coworker who is an executive with seniority? I'm not confrontational; my distrust and fear of people is still too strong at this point in my story, and I'm only just learning how to do the work of disentangling myself from these same ideological webs. I don't feel qualified to constructively pilot these conversations. My voice would shake and I wouldn't be clear and I'd just add to their idea of a naive, badly informed bleeding heart. I settle on a more covert, behind-the-scenes initiative: "losing" their suggestions in my inbox or simply prioritizing better messaging in our marketing assets.

For the most part, though, I'm happy in my new job because I feel like I'm genuinely an asset. There's a lot of room for me to bring my photography and marketing skillsets into play on their team and help them gain ground they previously weren't covering. It feels good to flex my professional muscles and see the brand benefit from my work. Slowly I feel my confidence starting to grow back.

After trauma, it's expected that your trust in other people will take a huge hit, but no one talks as much about how your trust in yourself can also evaporate. After your assumptions, instincts, and sense of safety are shown to be completely false and untrustworthy, you begin to think the same of the brain that misled you. Your brain.

I remember going to a young professionals' networking event not long after the Breaking. My bubbly, extroverted, unflappable best friend, Ashley, urged me to go. She said she'd come with me and that it might help me find a desperately needed new position. But the day came, and minutes before the event started, something came up and she couldn't make it.

Completely unmoored, I pushed myself to stay the course and go it alone. Walking in, knowing no one, I forced a hollow smile and felt totally invisible. I was so sure that anyone who did happen to notice me would see straight past my blazer and button-down and know me instantly as a fraud. In reality, everyone was very kind. But because their friendliness and inclusivity were discordant with my internal sense of self, I felt a strange guilt. Like I was lying to them about who I was.

I stuck it out as long as I could, then excused myself about fifteen minutes before the event officially ended. I hoped it would come across like I was very busy, a professional who's in demand. But on my way out of the room, the organizer of the event stopped me to thank me for coming. As I shook his hand, I saw movement in the corner of my eye. The muffin I had panic-bought but could not bring myself to eat was strewn in a wide trail of crumbs across the floor, and two kind strangers were kneeling to clean up my mess.

In my white-knuckled left hand was the lingering plastic wrap, nearly empty. Apparently, I had unknowingly pulverized the pastry in a vise grip as I fought to have a handful of small talk conversations.

It was so humiliating. With shaking hands I rushed to help the volunteer clean-up crew, but not before they had cleared away most of the mess. In my car I cried into my steering wheel. Ashley texted and asked how it went. "So good!" I replied.

Looking back on this pitiful scene, I feel very much like Pi did when he first locked eyes with a drowning tiger. If there really was no tiger, if it was only a projection of Pi's stronger self, then this bit of text is so full of self-compassion it makes me weak:

> "He looked panic-stricken . . . the water about him was shifting wildly. He looked small and helpless . . . . His nose and mouth kept dipping underwater . . . . He was looking up, taking in the sky one last time."

I wish I had been able to step outside of my skin and view myself like Pi viewed that desperate tiger when I found myself in that stormy season of self-distrust. Like that tiger, I was in an environment that I had never expected to navigate: tigers were not made for the open ocean, nor are they supposed to be caged and kept in the belly of a ship. In the same way, I could never have prepared for what hit me, nor should I have been put in that position at all.

There were so many factors actively undercutting my confidence during this time, but the reality was not that I was weak, or stupid, or cowardly, or broken. I was still every bit a tiger. I was just a little in over my head.

There were lots of painful moments like the muffin in the months and years following the Breaking. But I see now that all these moments were so important. It was critical for me to see that I could trust myself to get through them, all on my own.

This distrust of self is a hard, hard thing to come back from. It's a completely internalized battle. Only you can know if you're making progress. Slowly, however, I'm starting to feel like I'm getting somewhere, thanks in part to this new job.

———

As summer turns to autumn, I start making preparations for my first professional trip back to India. It's set to be a whirlwind with plans for me to shoot pictures and video in several Indian cities I did not get to visit on my last journey, including Bengaluru, Kolkata, and Chennai. Ever infected with insatiable wanderlust, Tim requests time off from work and is cleared by my company to travel with me for part of the trip. He's also given permission to share my company-sponsored accommodations if he agrees to work as my "second shooter." Essentially, he'll assist me and serve as a second angle photographer to ensure we get enough coverage of all the events we'll be attending. While I had mentally prepared to do this trip alone and will still have to perform the final half by myself, I'm super relieved that he'll be joining me. His presence anchors me.

The Indian visa system, on the other hand, is complicated and not timely; it seems like more than the railway system runs on Adnan's "Indian Standard Time." But right at the last minute, after weeks of jumping through hoops, I receive my new official Indian business visa.

Tim and I will spend several days shooting with a partner ministry local to Bengaluru before heading to Kolkata. There we'll meet up with the executive leadership of my company as well as representatives from a U.S.-based partner ministry. They're visiting India to see how their support of audio Bibles is impacting lives specifically in and around Chennai and Bengaluru, and my job is to help serve as host. The trip concludes with a multi-day conference in Delhi.

I pack and repack my substantial load of camera gear: one camera for still photographs, two cameras to capture video, four different lenses, two mics, one audio recorder, and a slew of cables, adapters, spare batteries, gear cleaning tools, and little packaged rain ponchos—they're great for throwing over gear in the event of sudden rain. I end up tetrising most of this equipment into my backpack. I'm happy to muscle it across the globe rather than check it on the flights in exchange for the peace of mind that comes with always having it in my line of sight. The remaining audio gear goes into a black equipment container called a Pelican case nested in my suitcase. Everything is ready to go, and yet, as our departure date draws closer, I develop something worse than cold feet; I feel like I've swallowed a block of ice.

It's a very long trip. The shooting schedule is ambitious. And the idea of traveling with VIP executives and client representatives and being "on" all the time makes my introverted brain quake.

At the same time, I'm aching to experience the warmness of India's people once again. To ride a tuk-tuk through the impossibly busy streets lined with perilous high wires. To bobble my head at friendly strangers. To have a real chai.

Now, seated once more in a cramped plane seat, I pull my headphones on and queue up the most positive, optimistic song I can think of. The original 1964 cast of *Hello, Dolly!* howl the words penned by Jerry Herman: "Put on your Sunday clothes, there's lots of world out there . . ."

As our wheels retract, I'm holding onto the tigress' tail with a death grip. This time, I'm electric with both nerves and hope.

10
Washing Machine Lassi

My hometown of Atlanta is nicknamed "the city in the forest." Maybe that is why Bengaluru instantly finds a place in my heart. Our first full day in the city reveals how the sprawling metropolis has grown and spread in between the trunks of trees—vast rain trees, sprawling ficus trees, majestic banyan trees. This is also a city in a forest.

Our hotel sits on a peaceful, heavily shaded road. When I say "peaceful," I mean that there isn't constant car horn honking, only occasional honking. It's a modest hotel, on par with an American Holiday Inn, and it's clean and comfortable. Our room overlooks a road where there's almost always a handful of dozy cows keeping motorists on their toes. At breakfast, Tim and I both ask for the biggest mugs of masala chai we can get. We sip them while we nibble on toast spread with orange marmalade. The bowls of berries and sliced apples look amazing, but we're back in India. Best to avoid any raw foods that could have been washed in water.

Once we've finished, we grab our gear and head out to meet Danesh.

Bengaluru born and raised, Danesh is the second-generation manager of an audio ministry that partners with the company I work for now. The building that serves as the home base for his work as well as his personal residence is just a short walk from our hotel. It's a narrow, four-story structure surrounded by a gated courtyard. Danesh meets us at the gate. A sleepy-eyed cocker spaniel dozing in the shadows of the ground floor greets us with a rumbly howl as we make our way to the second floor where Danesh and his team are just beginning their morning meeting.

Danesh is in his late thirties and has two elementary-aged kids with his wife, Anika. He left a prestigious position at an American tech company to take over for his dad, Arjun, who started the ministry. Back in the day, Arjun would haul bags of cassette tapes, each an audio recording of scripture translated into obscure Indian languages, to rural communities buried in the heart of his country. Sometimes he would have to travel for days by train, sleeping upright with the bag of tapes hugged to his chest, to reach the most isolated communities. Just to give them the chance to hear scripture in a language they could understand.

The ministry still maintains this analog tech, but now, under the leadership of Danesh, the team is anything but analog. He's partnered with ministries and companies like mine to find the best tech solutions to reach his ever-modernizing country. Our audio devices are great for certain communities he's serving (such as the visually challenged and the very rural) because the tech is solar-powered, water-resistant, and extremely rugged. The devices also have a built-in speaker so more than one user can hear the audio at a time. But this isn't the right solution for every Indian, Danesh and his team are finding. Our world is dominated by smartphones and streaming, and India is not isolated from this, so the company is also creating an app.

Tim and I sit with Danesh and his team as they perform their morning routine. Danesh reads a Charles Stanley devotional, and we sing a few Western worship songs. I'm still not used to prayers in my professional workday. I feel conspicuous, like an unprepared actor pretending to know my lines. My spirit is leaning elsewhere, trying to rush us all through the ceremony and toward the real work. The most important thing on my to-do list today is to capture video and photos of how an audio Bible actually gets recorded, and these rituals feel forced and in the way.

Finally, Danesh leads us down the hall to a room bisected into a sound booth and a recording panel. "Here is our recording studio." It's small but impressive. After you factor in the producer and the reader, there really will only be room for one person with a camera. That means either Tim or me.

Satvik, a member of Danesh's team with an award-winning smile, speaks up and offers to take Tim around Bengaluru on the back of his motorcycle to capture B roll—filler footage used to cut between interviews or other primary clips. I haven't seen Tim this excited by an idea in a long time, so I wave him off to explore with Satvik, grab my gear, and head into the booth.

In addition to audio Bible distribution, a large part of Danesh's work has been coordinating with other local Indian groups to get the Bible recorded in all the thousands of Indian languages and dialects. This is a more political process than you might expect as most translations of the Bible are protected under copyright law. Just like you could not record yourself performing "Yellow Submarine" and then list it on Spotify, many ministries and missionaries are barred from translating the Bible into a new language and then making it available for use.

This confused me when I first heard Danesh explain it. "The people who are holding the copyright—the ones who are not permitting the Bible to be made available in a new language—are Christians or Christian ministries?" I had to clarify. Yes, he confirmed, these people are the ones who, as they themselves would admit, hold the rights to the Word of God. Even if you don't believe the Bible is the Word of God, this seems like a stingy power play, especially when the copyright holders grant access to their version of the Bible to some ministries and not others—but they *do* believe it is the Word of God, and somehow that makes it even nastier.

We could give these copyright holders the benefit of the doubt and assume they are trying to protect "the fidelity of the canon" since they are not the ones who are doing the translating. I don't know. I just see how it all impacts Danesh and his team and the communities they serve.

Several different readers cycle in and out of the small studio speaking several different languages. In addition to scripture, we also have them record some short scripts that I'll use as voice-over in promotional videos meant for an Indian audience. By the afternoon, jet lag is hitting me like a wrecking ball. I feel myself nodding off in the close silence of the recording studio, broken only by the warm, melodic voice of the performer. I have to summon all my will and mental fortitude, but I make it through my first workday in Bengaluru, and it's a great feeling despite my fatigue.

Tim and Satvik return with helmet hair and flushed cheeks just as I wrap up the studio shoot. They make a fun duo: tall, broad-shouldered Tim with blond hair, blue eyes, and a big beard and dark-eyed, glossy-haired Satvik with a close-cut goatee and a trim, compact frame. I can only imagine what other locals must have thought about him buzzing around the city with a huge Viking on the back of his motorbike.

An expert guide, Satvik was able to show Tim interesting corners of the city, including the Islamic neighborhood where bearded men with strong arms and covered heads butcher huge cuts of meat (work that vegetarian Hindus would never do) and busy intersections dominated by yellow and green rickshaws blaring their horns. They even stopped to enjoy a coconut plucked from a huge pile on the side of the road, which they opened with the roadside salesman's machete so the sweet, tepid water could be easily sipped.

Tim and I make our way back to our hotel as the bats start to dip and weave in the twilight. I'm so exhausted, I don't even feel my head hit the pillow.

Day two. The most important day. I wake up early, before my alarm, already nervous about the next twelve hours. This is the heaviest work-day of the entire trip, with a jam-packed shooting schedule involving a dozen different local volunteers who will appear on camera and several different shooting locations. It occurs to me that there is a reason why film productions require so many people (and so much money). It's a lot of freaking work. I might have been overly optimistic about my own capabilities.

I try to remember all I faced on my last trip, all I claimed in so many different Indian and Nepali cities: the courage of Kathmandu, the anger and recovery of Agra, the peace of Tordi Garh. During our hastily eaten breakfast, I touch each memory in my mind, over and over like rosary beads, to try to summon a little confidence.

We walk around the block to Danesh's building under a deafening, droning noise. It almost sounds like the snoring man on the train from Varanasi. We heard it yesterday too but didn't think it would still be blaring after twenty-four hours.

"What is that noise?" I ask as Danesh opens the front gate for us.

"It is for the Hindus," he explains. "They must say so many *ooms* in their life, and they believe that if a recording of someone saying *ooms* is played on loudspeakers mounted all over the city, they can listen and it is like they themselves are saying it."

And it's just now that I can make out the super grainy, low-fi human voice rumbling a meditative "Oooooom . . ." again and again. Ultra-religious people, no matter what kind of church or temple or building they frequent, love a loophole. The *ooms* continue unabated from speakers mounted on signs, lampposts, and even the trunks of the giant trees for the entirety of our stay in the city.

Danesh goes on to explain the festival Vinayak Chaturthi, a Hindu observation that just happened not long before we arrived. I'm not sure if the *ooms* are part of this festival, but I have definitely seen remnants of the revelry in the large lake not far from our hotel. What I thought were just mounds of trash and refuse in the water (not uncommon, based on our previous travels around India) turn out to be many plaster idols of the elephant-headed god Ganesha. During the festival, household idols of the multi-armed god are dumped into the nearest body of water to release him back to his celestial home.

It makes a huge mess as the idols slowly deteriorate and leach chemicals and pollutants into the water system. Danesh says that these household idols can unofficially signify a family's status, so the bigger and more exquisite the idol, the higher its family's status. It reminded me a little of American Christmas decorations. What American will deny that our Christmas decor (whether it be outdoor light exhibitions or tall, perfectly manicured indoor trees) can also be a status symbol? Unfortunately for the lakes and rivers of India, Danesh says, bigger idols just make for a bigger mess at the end of the festival.

Our day quickly gets going when our first on-camera volunteer shows up. Shreya looks to be around my age, with big dark eyes and a warm smile. We cross off each shot of her with the audio Bible device on my shot list: Shreya using the device as she walks along Bengaluru streets. Shreya's hands holding the device. Shreya listening thoughtfully to the Bible in her native tongue. Finally, we come to the last shot I want to capture: Shreya using the device in a rickshaw.

We flag one down, and Shreya explains to the driver that we just want him to circle the block a few times. It's a weird request, and I don't have to speak Tamil to see that he's not asked this often. But he agrees, and Shreya and I pile in. She uses the audio Bible in the backseat as the city swirls around the rickshaw. The footage turns out perfect, and Shreya has such a good time that she stays for the rest of the day to help out with the other volunteers. The extra help, especially her ability to speak the local language, is a lifesaver.

After spending all day on our feet, we prepare to wrap our shoot. But there's one last shot I really want to capture: a time-lapse of traffic speeding by the camera. It's risky; it requires standing in traffic. For once Tim is the one urging caution, restraint—"Reconsider this idea." But it would represent quintessential India, and the tigress says to try. I promise to be quick, hand him my backpack, and face the busy street.

When locals cross the street here, they drip with confidence even as traffic rages around them. It's baffling. Somehow they make it across. I do my best to emulate them and begin my crossing. I make it through the first few lanes after a lot of wait-then-run, finally coming to the endpoint of a large cement partition that separates opposing directions of traffic.

Plastering myself against it, I set up my camera and monopod and hit record. Rickshaws, motorbikes, and the occasional car whiz by in lanes on either side of me. And I stand still, as still as I can, for as long as I can, until Tim and Shreya start gesturing wildly for me to come back to the safety of the sidewalk.

The girl that first landed in Kathmandu would've been dumbfounded.

Our last day in Bengaluru is gloriously unstructured. Originally it was planned to be a time for backing up SD cards and dumping footage onto hard drives, but that's already been done. Instead, we're in for a treat: Danesh and his family want to show us around their city.

They take us to one of their favorite biryani restaurants for lunch. Danesh orders for us, summoning all the best dishes. He shows us how to use our hands to make the perfect biryani bite, with tender meat, steamy rice, and just enough sauce. His favorite are the beef dishes, and he tells us about all the memorable burgers and steaks he's had on his visits to the States.

At the end of lunch, when the hostess brings me a bowl of warm water with slices of lime in it, his eyes glint, and he says, "You're supposed to drink it."

I hesitate at first. Is he . . . pranking me? His wife, Anika, catches my eye and shakes her head with a smirk. Over her shoulder I see other diners washing their hands in similar bowls. He *is* pranking me! My jaw drops at his cheekiness, but I smile too. Good friends prank each other, and I feel grateful to have crossed the barrier between colleagues to good friends. He laughs, I laugh, and the kids laugh at the idea of drinking hand-washing water. I feel perfectly at home.

We get lassi after lunch. A local shop has somehow rigged a top-loader washing machine to churn lassi in the big drum meant for clothes. The operator dips a ladle into the rotating drum and pours out cups of the thick dairy drink for us. I missed out on lassi in Varanasi and I still wound up sick, so I'm not about to turn down another opportunity. I opt to have some with fresh mango, despite that familiar spike of anxiety. Who else can say that they've had lassi out of a washing machine? If I get sick, at least it's a story.

And the fact that I decide this so quickly, almost subconsciously, is my biggest Bengaluru victory. It's such a small decision compared to others I've made on my journey, but sometimes the smallest decisions can reveal the biggest growth.

Before heading back to our hotel for the day, we peruse a collection of stalls and shops. The place is mostly filled with tourist trappings: scarves, cheap jewelry, and elaborately beaded, pointed, flat-soled shoes. But on one corner is a sari shop. During our first trip I developed such a love of saris with their bold, bright colors and dramatic sweeps of silky cloth. They're feminine in a way that I love—not in a fragile way, like a tiara or a tutu, but in a solid, confident way. Like a tigress. There's nothing quite like a sari.

Anika and I start chatting about the saris displayed in the front window, and she suggests we go inside, and maybe I could try one on? I fumble through an explanation of cultural appropriation, how I wouldn't want to thoughtlessly snatch up Indian culture like some kind of souvenir. But she smiles and opens the door. "It's an Indian dress, yes, but anyone can wear it."

I follow her inside. She speaks to the attendants and asks me what color I'd like to see. "Blue?" I suggest.

They pull out a deep royal blue fabric lined with four inches of intricate gold lace on the bottom. The store attendant wraps and plaits the fabric around me in mere seconds. The result is exquisite, and I'm completely smitten.

Anika grins. "Do you like it? It's very beautiful. And it fits perfectly; they wouldn't even need to tailor it."

"Yeah, I really do."

Tim, Danesh, and the kids join us and ooh and ahh over the blue sari. I beg Tim with my eyes and he responds like it's a no-brainer. "Get it! It looks amazing on you!"

I'm still not sure if it's the right choice, but I buy myself that royal blue sari, and I glow the whole way back to our hotel. And I wonder: how many other good things have I missed out on because instead of just asking for permission, I shoved a pre-written rejection in someone's mouth before they could speak?

Was I really afraid of culturally appropriating? Or was I just afraid to be rejected?

This habit of self-sabotage sprang from my fear of trust. Looking back, I can see its crooked roots running deep into the Breaking. I didn't want to trust someone long enough for them to reject me, so I beat them to the punch. I would step into an interaction already assuming that I didn't belong, that I was unworthy, that I was undeserving. It was armor. But armor is just a type of cage we elect to live in.

The soft, silky fabric of the sari between my thumb and forefinger feels nothing like armor and very much like a hopeful breeze.

Later that night I meticulously pack up each camera, each microphone, each lens. We'll leave Bengaluru early the next day and head for Kolkata (a three-hour flight) where we'll pick up the executives from another partner ministry. The main goal for the rest of this trip is to show these people the work that our organizations are doing together in India and strengthen our cooperative relationship. Their ministry also partners with Danesh and his team, so he and Arjun will be joining us for most of our excursions. We'll make our way northwest along the country, stopping in Chennai, Delhi, and Agra and covering almost four thousand total miles by bus, train, and plane. I have interviews and shot lists and audio recordings I'll be picking up along the way, but my top priority will be the comfort and experience of our VIP partners.

I'm tired just thinking about it all, but I also can't wait to see more of this country that's so thoroughly stealing my heart.

11
More Than Shadows

It's raining when we arrive in Kolkata. We get in late at night, and the slick streets are splashed with the reflected lights of cars and street lamps. Danesh will join us soon, but it was sad leaving the rest of our newfound family in Bengaluru: Anika, the kids, Shreya. And the trees. I miss the trees.

Unlike the arbor paradise of Bengaluru, Kolkata is thoroughly urban and claustrophobic. Tall buildings race up into the clouds. Cement overpasses crisscross over our heads, with large street communities burgeoning onto the sidewalks beyond their shadows. Our hotel is one of the buildings whose top is hidden by the low clouds.

This city has been significant to me since high school when I first saw the documentary *Born into Brothels* about a photographer who goes to live in the red light district of Kolkata. She originally intended to document the lives of the women living there, but it's the children that quickly become her focus. This documentary was my entire personality for a long time. It was one of the main reasons why I went to film school.

For so long Kolkata lived in my brain alongside Rivendell, Hogwarts, and ancient Egypt—I never expected to step inside any of them. Now, as I speed through her rain-wet streets, the world feels a little smaller.

Tim and I are thankful to wake up to a slow morning with no film-ing on our agenda. The rain still falls resignedly outside our window, and I can see right across the street under a cement overpass is another street community, dripping with rain and hemmed in with mud. Poverty living right next door to opulence.

We dress and head downstairs to a breakfast rendezvous with my company's executive management team and our VIP partners. My anxi-ety rattles around a little louder in my head now. These VIP partners are representatives from an old ministry, with old money and older leader-ship. I feel absolutely certain they are going to be judgmental, crushing fundamentalists. And probably all old white men.

But once again, my anxiety is wrong. They are all three women, from diverse backgrounds and with a wide age range. One in particular, Beth, knows the words to *Hamilton* tracks and speaks admiringly of Nike's recent advertising partnership with Colin Kaepernick—it launched not long after the NFL quarterback landed in hot water for kneeling during the national anthem in protest of racial injustice and minority oppression in America. The ad read, "Believe in something. Even if it means sacrificing everything."

The campaign is loathed by most conservative religious people who view Kaepernick's kneeling during the anthem as disrespectful. But Beth speaks openly in favor of the campaign. With just a few comments, she becomes a lighthouse cutting through my fog. A safe place.

Our group piles into a rented van and heads deeper into the heart of the city toward our main agenda item of the day. We find it nestled in an unassuming little backstreet. Without any fanfare, signs, or tourist trap-pings, we find Mother's House.

Crossing the threshold of a door right off the street, we step into a small, open-air courtyard lush with plants that look like peace lilies. There to greet us is a life-sized bronze statue of the Angel of Kolkata, and I'm immediately struck by how small Mother Teresa was. I'm a few inches over five feet, and the statue of Mother is still smaller than me.

Through the courtyard and into another room is her final resting place. It's a simple space that, I'd learn later, used to be the dining hall for the convent. Basic wooden benches and plastic chairs line either side of her long marble encasement. On top, a marker reads:

"Love one another as I have loved you."
- John 15:12
Mother M. Teresa M.C.
26.8.1910–5.9.1997
Dearly Beloved Mother
Foundress of the Missionaries of Charity

It's crazy to think that I walked the earth at the same time that she did. She seems like a larger-than-life figure who lived and died long before me. The evils she fought, too, feel like they should belong to a more primitive time, but I was two days away from my seventh birthday when she died.

As we all sit beside her, each of us in our own silent reverie, I pull up quotes attributed to her on my phone. I feel like this is a fitting way to honor her in the silence of my own mind:

"Find your own [Kolkata]. Find the sick, the suffering, and the lonely, right where you are—in your own homes and in your own families, in your workplaces and in your schools. You can find [Kolkata] all over the world, if you have eyes to see. Everywhere, wherever you go, you find people who are unwanted, unloved, uncared for, just rejected by society—completely forgotten, completely left alone."

My soul squirms. When I hold my life, my career up to the light and compare them to her words, do they match? Did I make the right choice when I decided to join a ministry, or was I meant to stay where I was? Breakfast suddenly doesn't sit as comfortably in my stomach.

Later that night, back in our hotel, our group meets in the lavish dining room for dinner. Four or five different buffet stations covered with a vast assortment of entrees, sides, salads, fruits, breads, and desserts are ready to satisfy our every whim. Attendants wheel in laden carts to restock and replenish as food is consumed. And outside our window, we can see the meager lights and blue tarps of the people living underneath the cement overpass.

I feel ashamed to be here, and helpless. Throughout dinner, I try to keep up a smile and chat with the rest of the group, even as I feel that shame laced up with depression and settling its heavy mantle quietly across my shoulders.

Many people struggling with depression do not choose to get help, and I understand why. Yes, sometimes depression feels like terror: a gaping, fathomless pit threatening to swallow you up, and perhaps during those times it's more obvious that we should seek help. But other times depression feels like a cocoon. Dark and small, but also safe. Isolated. Depression can lie and make you think that it's actually comfortable.

It's helpful for me to think of depression as a spectrum. It's not that I either have it or I don't. It's not a pass/fail test. It's one of the rhythms of humanity that everyone will experience at some point. Most of my life before the Breaking, I didn't hear it at all. After the Breaking, it was a relentless, driving, torturous cacophony that drowned everything else out. And at other times, like when I struggled to get a job, or when I reeled from a breakup, or after I graduated college, or even now, it has been a persistent, steady beat numbing me into oblivion. Into the cocoon.

Especially when you've been through a Breaking, the idea of marshaling effort to break that cocoon can seem painful, dangerous. And it is at first. As I worked to push out of that shadowy place, I often felt naked, cold, exposed. It would have been so much easier to stay in the dark.

But you have to set the broken bones. The longer you live in this fractured, constricted place, the more it will crystallize, fusing to all of you. And you are so much more than your shadows. You are every laugh that ever rushed from your ribs. You are every kind word and bold truth and sincere apology you ever spoke. You are every beautiful idea you've ever had. You are stardust and lightning and ocean spray. You are yesterdays and, yes, some of them may have been dark. But you are also a thousand tomorrows, and they are each brimming with golden promise. So object. Rage against the shadows. Like sunlight, love is bending itself at every angle just to reach your face.

At least, that's what I try to tell myself. I know that this is true, and I know that this is right. But there are still moments when I'm so overwhelmingly numb that it doesn't matter what's true or right. I can speak this over myself all day like a mantra—"You are more than your shadows . . . you are stardust . . . object." And sometimes it works. Sometimes I believe it. But the unfortunate thing about my depression is that even when I succeed, even when I feel like I've got this beast under control, I still find times when I'm slipping back into that small, dark space. And that's when it's the hardest to object to. Because it feels safe.

12
Those Who Have Not Seen

After an early morning two-hour flight from Kolkata, we land in Chennai, which at first appears to be just like the other bustling Indian cities I've wandered through: dusty, crowded, industrial, cramped. Then, after spending all day in an urban maze, we pull out onto a street, and suddenly there's infinite ocean under infinite sky. The expansiveness to my right in contrast with the congested city to my left is overwhelming, especially after spending the past eight hours indoors.

We have just finished hosting an event to give blind believers access to scripture in their "heart language" (the first native tongue they learned from their parents) of Tamil. Danesh and Arjun traveled from Bengaluru to help us orchestrate this hectic day in a borrowed chapel hall with no AC, where several different groups of visually challenged people and their families gathered to purchase their very own audio Bibles. One by one, we packed each group into the small sanctuary, sang together, and heard a brief message in their heart language from Arjun before breaking out boxes of audio Bibles. Rinse and repeat for the next group.

"We have them sign," Danesh told me as we set up before the very first group, "when they claim their audio Bibles. We use an ink pad, ask them to stamp their fingerprint on their order form, and this is their signature." I'd not considered this part of the process, but Danesh had. He knew many of the visually-challenged recipients today would have probably had a hard time signing to receive their ordered device, so he opted for an alternative that was both simple and incredibly beautiful. Instead of othering today's recipients by asking them to struggle through their signature or removing that step altogether, Danesh and his team created an efficient and equalizing alternative: Our signatures are unique, there's no two that look alike. So, too, are our thumbprints.

As we handed out the audio Bibles, we instructed people to wait, to open them after Danesh performed a brief tutorial. But no one in any of the groups ever did. They couldn't wait to turn them on. So, amidst the whir of electric fans circulating the hot air around us, dozens of "In the beginnings" and joyful exclamations in Tamil erupted from every corner of the room. One person would learn to navigate the keypad of their audio Bible, then turn to their neighbor and show them, and on it spread around the room. "In the beginning, God created the heavens and the earth . . . In the beginning, God created the heavens and the earth . . . In the beginning, God created the heavens and the earth . . ."

In the beginning, I believed this every day.

In the beginning, there was nothing that caused me to question whether this was true: that God was there, and that God created good things, and that God cared for creation. But now there are days when I don't believe. There are days when this is too good to be true. Some days, Death convinces me that it gets the last word. And this was one of those days.

Even without the resurgence of my depression, it would have been an incredibly taxing day. The endless excitement was emotionally draining, but it was also physically demanding work. Tim and I had to capture both photos and videos, so we were weighed down with multiple cameras and gear. Navigating the hot, crowded room, we bent and arched our bodies in whatever way was needed to "get the shot." As the last group of the day quieted to listen to Arjun speak, I slipped out the back doors into the churchyard. I just needed some air, and even though it wasn't any cooler outside, the atmosphere didn't feel quite so tight. Not quite so charged.

A short distance away from me kids tumbled over each other, barefoot and noisy. The very picture of unburdened childhood. In India it's common to see young children with *kajal* (a dark cosmetic makeup like eyeliner) around their eyes. Their parents will also sometimes apply black dots maybe the size of your pinky fingernail to a child's cheek. Almost like a beauty mark.

I asked Danesh about this. He told me both were meant to protect the child from "the evil eye," which was a concept that was totally foreign to me. I'd look it up later and learn that it's an old superstition claiming that an envious or malevolent glare could saddle you with terrible luck or misfortune. Even if you were unaware of someone looking at you this way.

Many of the kids in this little group had one or both of these types of evil eye protection. One of the older girls, the ringleader, caught my eye, and it wasn't long before all of them were pulling on my hands, telling me stories about each other in broken English, and posing for my camera.

I let them sweep me along in their games. A young guy emerged from a side building with a yellow Labrador retriever that couldn't have been more than a few months old, its ears and tail still floppy. He let me snuggle his puppy.

I could hear the team inside preparing to distribute more audio Bibles. I knew I needed to go back. That I would face yet another unrelenting wave of "In the beginnings," and my soul sighed.

I'd so much rather be outside in the sun, with the kids and the dogs.

We're traveling parallel to the ocean now because we're finishing our day with an impromptu trip to the historic Santhome Church. Later I would read up on this towering, pearly-white, angular building and learn it was built in 1523 by Portuguese missionaries. It's not until we get there that I realize that this is the final resting place of the apostle Thomas. Doubting Thomas.

Thomas spent many years in the land that we now know as India, ministering to its people and speaking of things he had witnessed before he converted one too many royals and was promptly impaled. I didn't know any of this until we were standing a few feet away from where he (supposedly) lies. Thomas, I think, would appreciate my general distrust of the whole relic scene.

Fun fact: when Jesus and the disciples learned that Lazarus had died, John wrote that Thomas basically said, "Well then, we might as well die too." If ever there was a disciple who understood life with depression, it was almost certainly Thomas. Maybe that's why the World Atlas describes him as "a pessimistic and bewildered man, yet one known for his courage." This makes me laugh because, honestly, I would be honored if that's how I am remembered someday. I know at least I've at least got the first half down.

Frankly, I think the church has fallen right into the same trap the disciples fell into when they argued about who should be called the greatest disciple. The church sorts and ranks and compares the twelve, and Thomas always comes dead last, just a little higher than Judas. And I just don't think that's fair. It all boils down to when he said, "Unless I see the nail marks in his hands, and put my finger where the nails have been, and put my hand into his side, I will never believe." But he wasn't the only one who needed to wrestle through some stuff in order to overcome doubt and find his belief.

After his resurrection, Jesus revealed himself to Mary Magdalene, who assumed he was the gardener who cared for the burial grounds. Even after having a conversation with him. She just couldn't believe it until he said her name. John and Simon Peter saw the empty tomb and abandoned burial clothes, and still they stayed hidden, locked away in a room with the other disciples. If you truly believed Jesus had risen from the dead, why would you hide yourself away? It wasn't until Jesus "came and stood among them [and] he showed them his hands and his side" that they believed. But Thomas was not with the other disciples when this happened. Pastors tend to leave that one little detail out.

As a "pessimistic and bewildered" doubter myself, I feel a kinship with Thomas. He makes sense to me. You have to remember, the crucifixion practices of the Romans were designed to maximize suffering and humiliation. It could take hours or days for victims to finally die. Now imagine watching your friend be crucified. Not wanting to witness their agony as the air is beat from their lungs, their humiliation as they are stripped publicly. Their hands raised in helpless defense. The shock of dark blood on their skin. Wanting to shut it out but also not able to look away, not able to leave them.

Hours of brutality, and you're utterly powerless to stop it.

What an unspeakable trauma.

If that same crucified friend were to suddenly reappear alive, wouldn't their scars be the first thing you'd look for? They would be for me. I don't think my mind would even stutter; my eyes would immediately start searching.

"Show me. Show me where they hurt you."

It's actually an incredibly intimate and empathetic response. I feel like Thomas is saying, "My friend, in his fullness, is too big to fake. So unless I see him with the entirety of his experiences written on his body, even and especially the brutality, I cannot believe it's him."

Jesus could've erased his injuries. If Jesus could come back from the dead, he definitely could have gotten rid of those gaping, grotesque wounds. The thoroughly ungodlike proof of his death. But maybe he knew that Thomas and the others needed to see them. Maybe he knew those wounds didn't just belong to him. That he wasn't the only one who suffered with each blow. Thomas and the other followers had also felt every one, all the way to their souls.

People like you and me, we've seen some crucifixions too. We've watched the crucifixions of our relationships, our futures as we hoped they'd be, even parts of ourselves. I think Jesus shows that when we emerge from that trauma, we don't have to have everything buttoned up and perfect. We don't have to erase our wounds or doubt. He essentially said, "Wounds are welcome here. I'll go first."

I don't think Jesus was criticizing Thomas when he said, "Because you have seen me, you have believed; blessed are those who have not seen and yet have believed." I think he was talking to me. He was reaching through centuries and talking about me, us. Those of us who can't touch his wounds for ourselves. But still, we endeavor to believe, and he called us blessed.

13
So-Called Strength

The fog of depression settles thick around me. I can't see the tigress anywhere.

Exacerbated by a lack of sleep, constant social interaction, and a long to-do list, I can feel myself slipping into depression compression. That tight space that feels hopeless and unending and cold.

On these days, if I was in my own home, I'd shut off my phone as soon as I possibly could before hiding away with a comfort read, walking my dog, or taking a nap. Over time, I've learned that being around people (in-person, on the phone, or via text) is not what I need when I'm in the fog.

But I can't do that right now. I'm in the middle of India, somewhere outside Chennai, for my job, on a bus with important people. And today is a very significant day. The last critical event of this entire trip is about to happen: another Bible distribution, this time in a very rural, underserved, overlooked community.

I know today is going to be just as emotionally taxing as the previous distributions, and my back aches thinking about it. It aches all the way through to the core of my spirit. Since I can't find the tigress anywhere, I make an executive decision for the sake of survival to wall up my overloaded emotions, seal them off, and try to tap into the ruggedness, the fierceness that I've seen in the tigress. Eyes ahead, mind set. I turn everything else inside me off.

After several hours on paved highways, our bus turns onto a dirt road, and the jungle greenery becomes denser in the windows. Eventually we park in a cluster of cinderblock buildings covered in fading paint. Dogs and barefooted kids trot around playing with each other, disappearing into darkened doors and reappearing to look at our van. This is an Indian "leper colony."

The first time I learned about leprosy, or Hansen's Disease, I was about twelve, and I was watching *Ben-Hur*. Why my parents let me watch this movie is beyond me. First, it's incredibly long. It takes approximately four years to watch in twelve-year-old time, and it has some incredibly disturbing images for a sheltered child, which I was. I mean, a guy gets trampled by a team of horses. They'll show that, but they won't show Jesus's face. And shrouded in mystery and horror, skittering through caves and dungeons, are lepers. The moment they're touched, they've doomed the person who's touched them.

This was the entirety of my understanding of leprosy for a long time. A lot of people, even in the educated West, still have approximately this degree of understanding of the disease, and it's incredibly inaccurate. In prepping for my trip, I spent several hours educating myself about leprosy—how it's transmitted, what its impact really is. Turns out Hansen's Disease is a bacterial infection. It's not spread through contact at all; it's actually spread through fluid from the face, like from a cough or a sneeze. However, most healthy immune systems can easily kill the bacteria. It dies so easily, in fact, that once it's sneezed out of someone's body, it expires quickly on any given surface. Even in controlled lab environments it's notoriously difficult to keep alive.

I once heard leprosy described by a medical professional as a "wimp of a pathogen." It's only ever really contracted by people with a weak immune system or a genetic disposition that makes them more susceptible. For someone living in poverty, whose immune system may not be supported by consistent, quality nutrition and/or is weakened from constantly combatting bacteria from a host of other sources, leprosy can pose a much greater threat. The bacteria that cause leprosy attack your nervous system, which robs you of your ability to feel. If you've seen pictures of people with leprosy, they may have been missing fingers, toes, or maybe entire limbs. This happens because they can't feel when they've burnt or cut themselves, and they can't feel when that wound then becomes terribly infected. The result is tissue loss.

This attack on the nervous system can also trickle down and create a host of problems like loss of eyesight, loss of cartilage, hair loss, and the inability to sweat—a potentially life-threatening condition in hot climates like India's. Despite a robust campaign by the Indian government claiming that leprosy has been eradicated within their borders, India accounts for more than half of all new cases globally every year. It's also one of the only places in the world that still exiles people (and their families) who contract the disease to rural "leper colonies," where they live out their days in poverty and isolation.

And it's curable. It's a completely curable disease. But there is so much misinformation about it and vicious social stigma that scientifically erroneous rumors persist. As a result, many people hide it once they've contracted it, failing to get help early before irreversible damage occurs.

In sum, leprosy is spread through poverty and cured through education. I am here to help with the latter. Stepping out of the car, I feel overtired and overwhelmed, but I straighten my spine, pull up my shot list, and get to work.

The team sets up in a small, one-room building with a cement floor and big, open windows in three of the four walls: the community's chapel. We're running almost the same agenda as our previous events: brief message from Arjun, distribution, tutorial. But afterward, the community will come together to enjoy a massive wok of chicken biryani made from supplies we've brought with us. It's enough to feed everyone in the community at least one hot, filling meal. "Man cannot live on bread alone" is an oft-quoted scripture passage, but it's obvious when I see this community that we certainly can't live only on scripture either. Even if it is in a heart language.

Fifty or so people gradually file into the little chapel room, leaving their shoes outside the door. The men sit on the left side of the room, the women on the right. There are no chairs, no benches, no pews. They all sit cross-legged on the hard cement floor.

As Arjun begins speaking, I watch the crowd from my place at the side of the room. Earnest, engaged faces, all of them. They bobble their heads responsively to the message. A majority of the attendees are missing one or more of their fingers. Some are missing significant portions of their feet. Some have sunken noses as the cartilage underneath has faded away. I feel anger boiling up inside me at the injustices they have faced, that they are still facing. This superfluity of suffering.

But what can I do? I can't fund and mobilize medical professionals to treat these withering bodies. I can't administer dapsone, rifampicin, and clofazimine, the trio of drugs that kills this insidious pathogen; I can't even pronounce them. There's nothing I can do, no place to put this seething anger. Better not to feel it. I douse the sentiment along with my other emotions. I wall it up as it threatens to flood my eyes with hot tears.

Our team breaks out the boxes of audio Bibles and begins passing them around the room. At the other distributions, recipients were charged for their Bibles; they were subsidized in a few particular cases, but most people paid. Danesh explained to me at the time that because so much aid is sent to India, people come to expect free handouts from ministries, and what ends up happening is they completely devalue whatever it is they receive because they didn't have to set aside funds or sacrifice anything to get it. For this completely impoverished community, however, our ministry partner—the company that sent Beth and her fellow VIPs—is covering the cost of their audio Bibles.

The devices are passed out, but unlike the previous distribution, it takes a little while for the first "In the beginning" to ring out. The loss of feeling in their fingers makes it tricky to know just how hard they need to press the power buttons to turn the devices on.

I'm still standing near the edge of the room, camera raised and ready to capture someone's reaction to hearing that first word of scripture, when one of the women reaches up and pats my thigh. I look down into her big, imploring eyes, see that her hands are not much more than a pair of palms. Small fingers, only a knuckle or two at the most, rim both. She lifts her audio Bible toward me and shrugs.

One of the women seated next to her grabs her hands and her device to try to show her how to turn the thing on, and I turn back to my viewfinder—a little grateful, if I'm honest, that an intimate one-on-one interaction isn't going to breach the seal that's keeping my soul protected.

But it's not long before she pats my thigh again. Her audio Bible doesn't seem to want to cooperate. I reach down and point to the power button and nod encouragingly to her. But she bobbles her head and adjusts her seated position so she's more directly facing me. Still holding out her device.

So, I let my camera settle on my hip and sink cross-legged to the floor in front of her.

Immediately the women next to her all scooch and rustle around on the floor to face me, making a little circle with their backs to the rest of the room. I take the troublesome audio Bible in my hand and point to the power button so everyone can see it. Even using my slightly trembling fingers with their glossy, albeit chipping, manicure feels obscene, insensitive. The little circle of women search for the power buttons on their own devices. I push this one hard, showing them how it must depress until it's flush with the keypad face. Then I hand it back to its wide-eyed owner and pull my camera around. Maybe I can capture her face.

With one hand I mime holding the audio Bible up to my ear, and she mirrors me, holding it up to her own ear. A second later the Tamil words ring out: "In the beginning . . ."

And she's immediately frozen. Her eyes lock on mine. She's so moved that all she manages to do is reach out and grab my hand, bare skin to bare skin, anchoring herself in this moment through me. She smiles, and her eyes get a little misty before she closes them. Still holding on to me. Still listening, enraptured, as if to the voice of a lover.

It's a moment that transcends religion and language and culture, and I'm swept up in it, my own eyes misting over too. The hastily built wall around my feelings dissolves under her touch.

I forget I have a camera in my other hand. I forget the baseless but nonetheless ingrained fear of her touch. I forget about my own wounds and insecurities and fatigue. All I do is sit in this moment that feels like the balm for every broken part of me.

How could I have refused it?

After that I'm unhurried. I spend time showing the women how to use their devices. They hand them to me one after the other, maybe wanting my presence and attention more than anything. Two things I am now more than happy to give them.

How could I have ever thought, here of all places, that turning my feelings off, walling myself up, was the way of the tigress? I mistook hardness for courage, numbness for ferocity. All the problems I couldn't fix overwhelmed me into thinking I couldn't fix any, so when I was asked for help, I failed to step up. I had to be asked twice.

Roshi Joan Halifax said in *Standing at the Edge: Finding Freedom Where Fear and Courage Meet*: "All too often, our so-called strength comes from fear, not love; instead of having a strong back, many of us have a defended front shielding a weak spine. In other words, we walk around brittle and defensive." *Brittle* is the perfect word to describe how I felt as our van rolled into this little village. Brittle, dry, fragile. Ready to shatter. "If we strengthen our backs, metaphorically speaking," Halifax goes on, "and develop a spine that's flexible, but sturdy, then we can risk having a front that's soft and open."

Or as Brené Brown so succinctly puts it in *Braving the Wilderness*: "Strong back. Soft front. Wild heart."

This. This is the way of the tigress.

We make our way back to Chennai and catch a train to Bengaluru. It's only been a few days, but I feel like I've been smashed and stretched outside the limits of the person I was when I was last there. The glow of my encounter with the afflicted women has worn off, and my old friend Depression has sidled back in, resentful I gave up her seat. And I left Bengaluru feeling so proud, so accomplished. I coordinated a video shoot, I even stood in the middle of traffic to get the money shot. Now all that momentum I built up has evaporated in the face of self-doubt and exhaustion and an overwhelming perceived helplessness in the face of suffering.

Our train ride is long, about five hours. The sun sets and transforms my window into a dingy mirror, reflecting back the face of the person I am least interested in seeing. The person who shut down, who checked out, who had to be asked twice. Who turned inward because she was so wrapped up in her own extraordinary lack of capacity.

But the relentless lights of the train car illuminate everything inside and render her unavoidable against the darkness of the night. Staring at my reflection, I'm so angry with myself. Disgusted.

"I'm still learning, still recovering," part of me defends itself.

"Why does everything always have to be impacted by this one stupid event in your life?!" My brain explodes in on itself in a flash of tiger stripes. "Why do you let it touch everything?!"

"It's not my fault! I just needed to rest!" If I'm honest, I'm not entirely sure which voice is me and which is the tigress. They've started to meld and swirl together, caving in on each other.

"Why can't you take responsibility for a bad decision? You walled yourself off. In a place where numbness causes disfigurement and death, how could you think that shutting yourself off was the right call?" I wish I could shove my own heart to the ground. I wish I could shake it.

"I just needed some time alone—"

"You don't get to pick and choose when you'll be asked to rise to the occasion! It's not going to wait until you're ready!"

"It might've been different if I'd had more rest."

"You don't know that. Maybe this is just who you are now: closed off, broken. How sad that in your own story, where you're meant to be the hero, you default to being nothing more than the victim."

Nothing more than the victim. I can't answer myself.

It'd be simpler to stay the victim. Victims hang back, sending the main characters along to fight the dragons on their behalf. Instead of owning the decisions that move their stories forward, they let themselves be rolled along by the decisions of other people, only moving when they must. Like me earlier today.

It's especially tempting to stay the victim when you have been truly, deeply victimized. What happened to you was tragic; not only that, it was completely outside of your control. What could you possibly have done to protect yourself? If you couldn't do anything before, how can you do anything now in your wounded state? It feels impossible to move on. Anytime someone acts as though the devastation shouldn't be debilitating, as though your victimhood is just something to be shaken off, you feel even more helpless. You can't just *stop* the hurt of the divorce, the absence, the injury, the death, the betrayal, the violence, the loss—and none of it is your fault. Why should recovery be up to you?

How can you even begin?

Please hear me when I say that yes, sometimes we need to be still, to pull away, to turn inward. Nurse our wounds, grieve our loss, guard against reinjury. But we also have to be honest and admit when we are refusing to face the pain of bone-setting that is required to heal. It isn't fair that we must endure this, and it's even more unjust that no one can do it for us. But it is the reality. Your life belongs to no one else, and you know yourself what you need to move forward better than anyone else. You may not feel like it, but you are the most qualified person for the job.

And it's work we can't avoid. If someone wants to be more patient, they must put themselves in situations that demand patience of them. Similarly, healing may require us to show up in situations that feel scary and abrasive. I can't deny how hard this is. But if I want to learn to trust again, I must practice trust. If I want to own my story, I have to show up to direct it. Even if I had no control over what happened to me, I do have control over myself. Over what I do next. Contrary to what my trauma tells me, I am not without power.

There is something powerful about connecting with others who have survived terrible things, particularly with someone who suffers *differently* than you do. And listen, I don't believe in the Trauma Olympics. We should never be competing for a gold medal in misery, and it's not helpful to tell someone in pain that they "should just be grateful because someone out there has it worse." But sometimes we need to hold mirrors up to each other so we can finally face what haunts us together.

This community in the wilderness outside of Chennai was full of suffering that looked nothing like my own. They know unfairness and pain and loss in a way that I will never understand. And yet meeting them, sitting with them, being seen by them helped me to understand my own suffering better. They helped me to realize that although I've seen growth since the Breaking, I'm clearly not finished. I must keep chasing down my own recovery and learn how to recognize when I'm letting my injury, not my heart, call the shots.

The truth is that no one can force you into recovery because no one can work your recovery for you. You are the hero you need, but no one can turn a victim into a hero except for the victim themselves. Maybe that's why so many of our favorite heroes have scars. They were victims once too but decided that was not how their stories were going to end.

It's up to me to decide how I respond to trauma, who I will be. This feels like bad news, especially after today. But I realize it's actually good news: there may be a lot outside of my control, but this is something that lies squarely in my hands, and my hands alone.

It's up to *me*.

14
The Gamble

When we arrive in Bengaluru, we bid Danesh and Arjun a bittersweet goodbye and head to the airport. Tim says goodbye too not long after. From here he is homebound, heading back to his office job and our own little Western corner of the world. His leaving feels to me like the loss of a lifeline, and it's murder for him too; he hates to miss out on anything. In all the ways this trip has drained me, it has filled him up, and he feels shortchanged to leave now. Reluctantly he boards his plane to Doha, where he'll board a second, longer flight to Atlanta. He's staring down twenty-five total hours of travel.

I board a different plane and prepare for less than three. I'm accompanying the executive team and ministry partner VIPs to the final stop on our itinerary: Delhi, punctuated with a day trip to Agra to see the Taj. The hardest work of the trip for me is over, but it's completely emptied me. I feel like a dead leaf, unmoored, about to float away. But I've made it this far; I can finish this trip.

Once my group has checked into our hotel, we meet up for dinner with the rest of the employees from the Delhi branch of my company along with some additional regional partners. Among them is a woman named Kohima. She looks to be in her thirties or forties, with straight dark hair cut in a straight line at her collarbone. Her eyes are upswept, more almond-shaped than most Indians' I've seen.

"My family is from Nagaland," she tells me. Nagaland is an Indian state in the northeast part of the country, next to Myanmar. "My ancestors were headhunters."

And I believe that. She looks like she's descended from warriors. She walks with her chin lifted, proud but not in a cold way. Her smile is contained, understated. But she's quick to make a joke. You can tell by the way she glances at you sideways that she's joking with you. Always followed by a friendly head bobble.

Kohima founded a company that employs former sex workers. They can come and learn how to make textile products like saris, bags, accessories, etc., which makes it easier for them to navigate out of the world of sex work. She's doing amazing things to empower people in need, and I quickly develop a crush on her. Even more so when she hands me a bag stamped with the logo of her business.

"I heard you like saris," she grins, gently leaning over to push her shoulder into mine. Inside the bag is a lush burgundy and gold fabric. A sari. It is such a thoughtful gesture from someone I hardly know, I'm taken aback. I would later learn that she doesn't live in Delhi but in Bengaluru and is good friends with Danesh and Anika. They must have told her about how I had gushed over saris.

This type of sari, she shows me, isn't just a length of cloth like my blue one. The women she employees have stitched in such a way that I can easily fasten it around my waist, and the cascading pleats and folds characteristic to the front of a sari easily fall into place. I don't need to refold them after every bathroom break. I try (and probably fail) to convey the depth of my gratitude.

———————————

I wake up at 4:00 AM the next morning. Our bus isn't leaving for Agra and the Taj until 5:30, but I need extra time to shower and get ready. If there was just one place on this great wide earth I'd want to wear a sari, it's at the Taj. So I'm going for it.

I unfold my blue one. It's the first one I fell in love with and, if I'm going to do this, I want to try to do it the authentic way. No shortcuts.

It's still dark outside. Whatever sunlight might have gradually peeked over the horizon is swallowed by smog. Even though I watch the YouTube tutorial over and over, I can't get the pleats in the front quite right. Eventually, I come close enough. The whole ensemble feels untrustworthy, like it could unfold into a puddle of fabric at my feet at any moment. I grab a pair of navy leggings and shimmy them on under the skirts. If my clumsy plaits decide to betray me, at least I won't be stark naked underneath.

The bus journey from Delhi to Agra is four hours. I try to sit as still as I can so as not to disrupt the sari. *Just hold for one picture I can send to Tim,* I silently urge the fabric. Tim is still in the air and unreachable by text, but I know he's still kicking himself that he wasn't able to stay longer. I just want to send him one decent photo and let him know I missed having him here too.

About two hours outside the city, our bus rumbles to a halt in front of a rest stop. And it's quite the rest stop. This isn't like the little lunch spot we stopped at all those months ago outside of Kathmandu: this has Western toilets and a Starbucks. As tight as I've got my legs crossed, I feel the inevitability in my whole body. I can't sit through another two hours on the road without hitting the bathroom first. My sari is doomed.

From the parking lot to the coffee stand, the rest stop is covered with people. Tourists and locals alike queue for drinks and stretch their legs in the dusty morning. As I enter the ladies' bathroom, a large group of women chatter and preen in the mirror. I squeeze past them and into the first available stall.

Staring at the toilet, hopping up and down a bit, I frantically try to figure out the best way to do this. I could have just lifted up my skirt if I hadn't had the bright idea to put on leggings. Disrupting my waistband in any way threatens to undo all the pleating, all my hard work because that's what is holding the bottom half of the sari together.

But there's just no way around it. And, as expected, all my carefully folded plaits gracefully slide to the nasty floor wet with unidentifiable liquid and strewn with tracked-in dirt and toilet paper. What a disaster. I should've just worn Kohima's sari. Afterward, cramped in my stall, I try to reassemble myself as best I can. I try to tuck and fold the slippery silky fabric back into the elastic of my leggings. But when I slip my thumb into the right side of my waistband, it creates enough space to undo all the tucking and folding I just finished on the left side (and back and front). In all my sighing and frustration, I don't even notice how quiet the bathroom's become in the absence of the other women.

When I'm halfway satisfied, I open the stall door and look into the eyes of my reflection. The mirror above the sinks on the opposite wall tells a disappointing story. Uneven, sloppy pleats are bunched around my middle. The whole thing hangs off me like a frown. At least I'm the only one here to witness it. No, wait, there's someone in the stall a few down from mine. But otherwise, it's just me and my frumpy sari.

In that moment, as I stare resignedly into my own face, a familiar feeling wraps itself around my core. The same feeling I felt when I wore a blazer and pulverized a muffin out of panic. The same feeling that almost kept me from accepting the job that got me here.

You're a fraud, a poser, an outsider, a fool who strayed just a little too far out of her own depths.

The opening of a stall door makes me jump, and I frantically pull the strings attached to the corners of my spirit to try to right it. Try to look like I belong here.

A woman emerges from the stall, locks her eyes on me through the mirror as she walks to a sink and washes her hands. I feel it. Even though I don't ever look up from washing my own hands, I can feel her constant stare. She looks away finally when she reaches for paper towels, and I loosen my breath. Relieved, as if I've escaped the heat of a spotlight.

She starts to walk toward the door, and I lean a little bit closer to the sink so she can pass by me, effortless in her own flawless sari of olive green and mustard yellow. But she stops right next to me and leans into my line of sight, her eyes searching ruthlessly for mine.

I meet her eyes, startled with dripping hands, and take a step back.

But in doing so, I reveal the extent of my incompetency. Her unblinking eyes sweep over my sari—my lumpy blunging waistband, my dirty, uneven hem. Now it's her turn to take a step back.

That one move, so small, wrecks me. I might as well be naked.

But then she steps forward, and her hands are on my shoulder, where the end of the sari fabric is swept up and over. Without a word she pulls it off and leans in close to pass it from hand to hand behind my back, unwrapping my skirt. I'm frozen to the floor.

Draping the fabric over her left forearm, she pulls every single yard off of me. She glances curiously at my leggings, which are definitely not normally worn under saris, before she takes an end of the fabric in her right hand and starts to redress me.

She presses her fingers on my hips, and I spin, understanding her silent instructions. I can smell the tang of sweat on her as her arms lift and work, that unpleasant but utterly human scent that she's probably smelling on me too, leaning in so close. Her hands masterfully plait the fabric and somehow secure it to my body. Then she sweeps the final few yards gently over my shoulder.

I turn to look in the mirror, a completely different garment on my body, and notice she's patting herself down. Like she's feeling for something in her own sari. She cranes her neck to look down at her right shoulder, her fingers fidgeting under the folds resting there. And she pulls out a safety pin. Her safety pin.

The fabric on her shoulder comes out of place and slips down her arm. But she smiles at me with a slight head bobble and reaches for my shoulder again, where she pins the last sweep of my fabric in place before stepping back to admire her work.

I'm speechless, which doesn't really matter. We don't speak the same language anyway. All I can do is smile and bobble my head as earnestly as humanly possible. She bobbles back, grinning, bringing her prayer hands to her heart, and sweeps out of the room in a rustle of silk.

The woman in the bathroom taught me that this tension of becoming a main character doesn't just involve a wrestling match between two warring versions of myself. Yes, I have to make the initial decision to get up out of the dirt; no one can do it for me, and sometimes I hold myself down. But there's also a struggle between the main character—the tigress—and the people around me.

For some trauma survivors like me, learning to trust people again is a grueling, always-scary process. Before, I trusted completely. I went all-in, pushed all my chips to the center of the table, and lost it all in that one cataclysmic event. Then slowly, ever so slowly, I regained some of that lost currency. But now betting anything after such a loss feels like too much of a risk.

Just like with gambling, however, the only way to gain more is to risk more.

Main characters never, ever exist in a vacuum. They have to have help: guides, sidekicks, mentors, teammates, spies, coaches, friends, allies. And protagonists have to trust those players because there will always be moments for the hero when they will be a bit too far out of their own depth.

Being out of your depth isn't an indicator of your ineptitude; it's an indicator that you are brave enough to take a risk, and taking risks is part of the work of recovery, part of rebuilding a life within community. Even if you own the main character role in your story—even if you're a tigress—you can't do this on your own.

This is the lesson India, God, humankind, the universe—you name it—has had to teach me over and over and over again. In an airport in Kathmandu. In a boat on the Ganges. In a side street in Tordi Garh. In a hotel in Kolkata. I have to relearn constantly that my anxiety, my fear, my failures, my depression, and my doubts are all valid—but they are never the whole story. And I do myself and my story a disservice by painting all the people around me as untrustworthy based on my old wounds.

There are still people out there who are worth the gamble.

I get the picture at the Taj thanks to my friend in the bathroom. Not only that, I get so many comments and selfie requests from locals. Their warmest, most welcoming embraces. One mom with her young son on her hip comes up to me, cups my face in one hand, and says in broken English, "Our culture looks good on you!" Too gracious. Too loving.

Across the globe Tim gets home. He's aching for a shower and his own bed, but he ambles to our mailbox and pulls out the backlog. After he's brought in all his luggage, he starts rifling through the bills, flyers, junk . . . and he stops when he sees an image of the Taj Mahal.

A postcard. The one I entrusted to a young bellhop six months ago in Jaipur on the advice of Adnan. It arrived into Tim's hands the same day, almost to the hour, that I was there without him.

Worth the gamble.

15
A Family Affair

I finish the conference in Delhi and turn my face toward home, ready for the long journey. Walking through my front door is just as sweet this time as it was after our first trip: here are my books, my dog, my bed, my fireplace. My husband. The shoulders of my soul sag in relief.

The weeks that follow are therapeutic. I settle back into my routine in my own safe little space, logging footage and photos from my recent trip. But it's not long before India beckons once more.

My father is recruited to be a board member for the nonprofit sister charity of my company. Just a few months from now all the board members will be flown to India to experience the impact of audio Bibles there—and, if they want, family members are welcome to join them. Now nearly my whole family will get to experience India firsthand.

This is a big deal. For months they've been hearing crazy stories about honking traffic and streetwise cows and piping hot chai; I couldn't have primed them better for adventure. My two brothers, one in high school and one in college, are well-traveled for their ages, but there's nowhere on earth like India. Culture shock for both them and my parents is all but guaranteed.

This trip is a big deal on a corporate level too: it could help secure additional funding that would be used specifically in India. So even though it falls outside of my marketing job description, I spend the next few months assisting the travel team and working closely with Danesh to create itineraries, book flights, coordinate transportation, and schedule activities. Remembering the mistakes I made in previous jobs, I still try my hardest to hold good boundaries within yet another company culture that seems mostly unfamiliar with the concept. It's shocking how quickly I almost slip back into my overworked, never-say-no inclinations. "But," I tell myself, "this job is not me, and I am not this job." Every time I hold my boundaries, it gets a little bit easier.

For the third time in ten months, I'm driving to the international terminal of the Atlanta Hartsfield-Jackson Airport. This time not just with Tim but with my parents and two younger brothers as well. Tim and I encourage them to stretch their bodies in all the ways you can't on a plane before we board.

"Once you're eight hours in," we tell them, "you'll wish you'd stretched your legs out."

Fourteen hours after takeoff, we reach Qatar. From the plane window we can see nothing but desert stretching to the horizon—except for right in the middle, where the incredible, improbable, man-made oasis of Doha shimmers like a lake of molten silver poured out on the sand. We land just as the sun starts to make its rippling descent into the dunes.

In the Doha Hamad International Airport, you can see humans dressed in nearly every conceivable fashion. Adventurous Europeans with high socks, big hiking boots, and bigger backpacks. Elegant African women in their colorful, starchy *bazins* and matching head scarves. Probably the most eye-catching, for me at least, are the Qatari men in their floor-length white *throbes* with red and white patterned *shemaghs* draping from their heads around their shoulders. They look beautiful, dignified, but I can't imagine moving and walking and living in a desert dressed in anything that concealing and claustrophobic. At least their clothing is primarily white. Most Qatari women—many of them also ambling about the airport—dress in a floor-length black *abaya* with a *niqab* covering their heads. I imagine those are even hotter.

I follow a few women dressed this way into one of the airport bathrooms and start to bring myself back to life. I brush my teeth and hair and liberally apply dry shampoo. I wash my face and swap my socks and my sports bra for a clean set.

My body thinks it's about 9:00 AM, albeit after a night of terrible sleep that's left me not exactly rested and ready to take on the day. When we land in Kolkata, it'll be about 2:00 AM local time. If I can just force myself to stay awake for the entirety of this next five-hour flight, I can get a leg up on jet lag. I'll collapse into sleep when we get to our hotel and wake up that much closer to aligning myself with my new time zone.

My family and I sip hot cups of coffee made in the Turkish style praying they'll keep us awake, and munch on the best falafel wraps I've ever tasted—that's not an exaggeration. As we approach the gate for our next flight, the travelers around us start to show a little more skin than their Middle Eastern neighbors. They become a little noisier too, a little more direct with their eye contact, and I smile as I feel India pulling me closer.

India. With her warm, welcoming, bold people who will unashamedly stare at you. Who have no qualms about loudly confronting a fellow passenger in a string of words that tumble headlong over their tongues. Who don't think twice about undressing and redressing you in a rest stop bathroom.

Maybe it's because I'm coming off weeks of much-needed rest in my own home, but for the first time, I stow my carry-on and buckle my seat belt without feeling like I have a vise grip on the tigress' tail. For the first time I feel like I'm pumping my arms, chasing after her on my own two feet.

—————————————

This comparatively quick, eight-day trip starts in Kolkata. All of the places we will be visiting are places that Tim and I have been before: Delhi, Agra, and Bengaluru. But our first stop is Kolkata and Mother's House.

The pacing of this trip is much slower than my last trip; the top priority is the comfort and experience of the executives and board members. We take our time, allowing them to savor each experience in India, including Mother's House. It's a warm, sunshiny day when we visit, so the cool of the courtyard and of the room where Mother rests is a relief. This time, mounds of orange marigold petals rest on top of her marble coffin, shaped to spell out, "Love begins at home."

It was only a few short months ago that I first visited this sacred space. I remember how it sent me reeling. Now as I watch the faces of other visitors around me, it looks like several of them are impacted just as deeply. I could be projecting, but I silently send kind thoughts their way just in case, hoping that whatever painful stretching their soul is experiencing grows them. Helps them find their tiger.

We enjoy lunch in the city, in the upstairs room of a bougie restaurant, and I tell everyone to try sweet lime sodas. When the hand-washing bowls of warm water and limes are brought out, I try to pull the same prank on my brothers that Danesh attempted on me. They've learned all my tells, it seems, so they don't fall for it. After lunch, we stop by the Victoria Monument before heading to the airport to catch our flight to Delhi.

Our first day in the capital city is spent entirely on touring and shopping. We take the board members to haggle in artisan villages, see the Lotus Temple, and walk under the India Gate. It's at the last that we spot a snake charmer, the first I've encountered in all my time in India: a man squatting down in front of a shallow basket, blowing into an instrument as a swaying cobra emerges.

I read that the practice was made illegal in India in 1972 because of the brutality required to render the cobras safe. The snakes are ruthlessly defanged; alternatively, in some cultures, their mouths are sewn shut, leaving an opening just big enough for their tongues to flick in and out. They eventually starve to death or succumb to infection of their stitches. Sometimes they are kept locked up in small, dark containers for over a month so their dehydrated muscles cramp and make them sluggish during the performance.

It makes my stomach churn to look at the pitiful wobbling animal, and I'm pretty sure I'm one of the only onlookers who cares. On top of the innate biological aversion all mammals have when looking at a poisonous snake, Christians tend to have a deeper, implicit hatred of snakes. Our culture often uses the reptile to symbolize sin, temptation, and evil. Satan appeared in the form of a snake to tempt Eve in the very first book of the Bible, and in the last book of the Bible, Satan is again referenced as an ancient serpent. Hence, I'm not sure lecturing my group to look away on behalf of the poor creature would be effective. The unfortunate little cobra is battling thousands of years of bad press.

It doesn't matter. The man doesn't stick around for long. As soon as a watching crowd starts to draw attention to his illegal scheme, he scoops up the basket and disappears.

We return to the bus to sit in standstill traffic. People approach our windows. This isn't unusual; peddlers selling water, flowers, food, etc. will often try to take advantage of this uniquely captive audience. There's really nowhere to go when you're stuck in bumper-to-bumper Delhi traffic.

This time, though, we're approached by two transgender women. They are just begging spare change, their thin hands lifted and cupped, both covered in dust from the road. One keeps pulling the end of her haggard sari up over her shoulder just for it to slip back down into the bend of her elbow again.

It's not possible while I'm stuck on the bus, but I want to help her pin it, like the woman in the bathroom did for me.

I've seen transgender women in India just one other time, when we first visited Bengaluru. They were begging on the side of the street as we passed by in a rickshaw. Danesh explained to us that to be a *hijra* (a transgender woman) in India, you face incredible persecution. People will not hire you. Most doctors will not treat you. You can be evicted from housing and excluded from receiving an education. Most people in this community have had to resort to living on the street, eking out a living through begging and sex work.

It makes them incredibly vulnerable to violence, sickness, and exploitation.

"It's very sad," Danesh finished somberly. "Very, very sad."

Now, as I watch the women move from window to window, someone in our group starts to make jokes at their expense. And something inside me snaps.

Ineloquently, imperfectly, I parrot what Danesh told me all those months ago in Bengaluru, loud enough for the whole bus to hear. I'm not yelling, but I'm much more forceful and confrontational than I've ever been with these colleagues before.

More than I've been with anyone in months, maybe years.

Maybe ever since my Breaking.

But I'm honestly not even thinking about that. I'm not thinking about where I fall on the org chart compared to the positions of my listeners or whether I'm qualified to be hijacking the conversation in this way. I'm just thinking about all the other times (and there were many) that someone solicited our group for money and were instead treated with respect. Or, at worst, indifference. Not once did anyone's behavior in our group degenerate to open scorn or mockery. Until now.

The joker goes quiet. A few people laugh nervously. And we leave the women to try their luck at another windshield.

For the rest of the day, I feel sick. I resent the fact that I was put in this situation, and I feel guilty that I'm more preoccupied with the sensations in my own soul and body than with the trans women. Thinking back, I can't even recall their faces. How can I not remember their faces?

I'm also unnerved by how quickly, how instinctually, I reacted.

When we landed in Kathmandu on my first trip and a blonde Australian made eyes at my husband, I said nothing. When I was incredibly sick on a train and a man asked to trade bunks with me, I acquiesced. Every other time coworkers and Christians in my circle have made troubling comments about this place and people I've come to love, I sidestepped them.

I didn't even say anything about the snake just a few hours ago.

What has suddenly changed in me? Adrenaline buzzes in my veins, and I second-guess myself from all angles. Did I go too far? Did I just put myself on an executive's subconscious "list"? Did I blow my opportunity to earn the confidence of this group? Did I undermine my message with my behavior? Did I do that stereotypical white woman thing where I presume to speak for a minority from a place of privilege?

Or did I not do enough? Should I have done more?

I know there was no way the trans women could've heard me, not over the incessant honking and whirring of idling engines, but still I worry that maybe I said something inaccurate, something that would have made them feel more ostracized. I worry I'm doing it now, in these pages.

And I wonder: maybe this is what it really feels like to take a stand. To finally be running shoulder to shoulder with the tigress.

It's not some romanticized, slow-motion moment where you're completely in the know and say everything right and the problem gets fixed. It's opening your mouth and being just as startled as everyone else to hear a tiger's roar.

It's shaky hands and adrenaline and second guesses and running ahead anyway.

On our second day in Delhi, the board members and their families attend meetings and special events specifically for the Delhi branch of the company and our ministry partners. Danesh and Anika fly in to attend, as does Kohima and her husband. These incredible people, with their boots on the ground, are the metaphorical midwives of our work, directly invested and committed to the communities they serve. They don't just talk a good talk. These tigers are living it. I delight in introducing them to my family.

The following morning everyone piles into a massive bus at 7:00 AM to set out for the Taj Mahal. I think back to that still-queasy girl who visited the Taj Mahal after a torturous, angry train ride. I wonder what she would have said if I had told her she would see that iconic dome two more times before a year had even passed.

My brothers are an absolute hit with the crowds at the Taj. Tall and beautiful, with dark hair and eyes, they are constantly approached for selfies. They're great sports about it, acquiescing and posing with anyone who asks. I was eight when Ethan was born, and twelve when Josh arrived, so in a lot of ways they are like my own kids. It makes me proud to watch them acclimate so gracefully to this place I've come to love, especially considering how rocky my own landing was when I first stepped onto this continent.

We move our operation to Bengaluru the day after the Taj to learn more about the work that Danesh and his team are doing there. His kids run out to us once we're inside the walls of their compound, and their cocker spaniel greets us with that same rumbly howl. Tim and Satvik link back up, two peas in a pod. It feels like a homecoming.

We aren't staying in our usual hotel this time; because of the status of the executives and board members, we check in to a much nicer luxury hotel in the heart of the city. Truth be told, though, I miss our old spot. It was our home for several days the last time we were here. Similar to the hotel we stayed at our first time in Kolkata, the wealth displayed in this new Bengaluru hotel feels vulgar and garish, especially considering our agenda for the following day.

Danesh and his team pick us up the next morning, and we turn our sights to the rural land beyond the city limits. We're participating in two audio Bible distributions today in two separate communities of people living with leprosy several hours away from Bengaluru. This is the most important day of the trip as it will enable board members to see how their support and dedication is impacting real people here in India.

The first community is a little collection of buildings set back off the highway and nestled in the shady jungle trees. The residents meet us as soon as we pull up with wide smiles and head bobbles. From where we parked our van all the way to their main meeting area, the dirt foot paths are covered in intricate chalk designs: the community's way, Danesh explains, of welcoming us.

They usher us into a covered cement pavilion and provide plastic chairs for the executives to sit in. Some of the children perform a dance they've prepared. Most of the kids that live in these communities are not afflicted by leprosy; it's usually one or both of their parents. Leprosy is not hereditary and cannot be transmitted in vitro or through breastfeeding. But because social stigma and misinformation about the disease are so prevalent, the children, parents, and siblings of someone with leprosy are outcast to the same degree as the person infected. Danesh explains this to some of the board members who are puzzled over the apparent health and vibrancy of the kids, especially the talented young dancers.

Tim and I orbit the space, capturing photos and videos so the other people in our group can put away their phones and cameras and be fully present in the moment. Then the audio Bibles are brought out, and the board members distribute them by hand. Just like in every other distribution, the devices are immediately unboxed and turned on.

All the board members are profoundly moved by the experience. I can see it on their faces through my camera's viewfinder. I can feel the emotion crackling like static in the air. Having had this overwhelming experience myself just a few months ago, I feel how good it is to consciously play a supporting role as they move through the same story. I do my best to capture photos of their meaningful interactions so they can remember the people they met in the wilderness of India.

The second community is further out, where the landscape becomes more arid, and is built close to the highway. It cascades up into a steep, windswept hillside with dozens and dozens of stairs connecting the various huts and buildings. The residents have chalked up their pathways too, and as we disembark from our van, we hear loud bangs and sizzling close by—so close we initially think something is wrong with the engine of the vehicle. Turns out the residents are so thrilled to host us, they set off fireworks as part of their welcome.

The distribution in this second community is very much the same, with the overload of emotion and the excited breaking-open of audio Bible boxes, but because this is our last stop of the day, we're able to go a little more slowly. We take our time with the residents who live here, Satvik and Danesh translating between the two groups of people. They welcome us into their homes. They proudly show us their livestock. One man grins and holds up a black and white spotted baby goat for my camera, giving it an affectionate kiss on the flat of its small cheek.

As we prepare to leave, the huge wok of chicken biryani we brought (as we did for the first community) becomes hot and fragrant. The wok is bigger than my bath tub at home, so everyone in the community will get at least one great meal. We leave them to enjoy it and load into our bus.

Some of the board members are in tears as they settle into their seats. I get it. I know that particular kind of overwhelm: the joy, the guilt, the gratitude . . . the tsunami of feelings that threaten to drown a person after an experience like this. The experience of reaching through the fog of a language barrier, distance, age, diametrically different life experiences, to find connection with another human being. Someone who just happened to be walking around on this earth at the same exact moment as you.

Against all odds, you were gifted a meaningful moment together.

16
Flow in the Frantic Storm

Our group parts ways in Bengaluru. Everyone hugs and thanks Danesh and Anika, grateful for their hospitality and leadership during our trip, before we head back to our homes in Switzerland, Canada, Israel, and for me and my family, the United States.

I settle into a luxurious seven-month stretch where I'm mostly working from home, occasionally boarding short domestic flights for conferences. These gatherings would become the most challenging part of my job—not from a professional or logistical standpoint, but because of where I stand spiritually and ideologically. They are a concentrated three-day dunk into the world of American evangelicalism, and nearly everyone who attends has an axe to grind. Televangelists, Christian film-makers, a man who dresses up as a Roman Praetorian Guard and recites his version of some Bible story: all the weirdest flavors in Christendom converge. Each time I attend another event, my forbearance inches closer to its maximum limit.

One of these conferences is held in the same place and at the same time as WonderCon, a super nerdy fantasy convention, and the contrast between the attendees of both groups is surreal. In one ballroom I spy Transformers, superheroes, and scantily clad fairies; in another, nothing but a sea of button-downs, khakis, and combovers. The shared spaces of the lobby and hallways look like a crossover episode between *Seinfeld* and *The Witcher*.

I catch sight of a young woman in a seriously impressive costume of one of my favorite fantasy characters, so I start to approach her with compliments locked and loaded. But then she turns around. She's on the phone. "Honestly, it's so bizarre," I hear her say. "I don't know who thought it was a good idea to schedule these at the same time . . . I know, and there are so many MAGA hats . . . these people are crazy."

And immediately, I feel the loneliness that occurs when you don't belong over there, and you don't belong over here. You're floating somewhere in the middle.

I don't talk to her. I don't tell her how much I like her costume or that I agree with her (and that she doesn't know the half of it). I just go back to work. And when I get back to my company's booth, I walk into a very heated conversation between some coworkers and a few conference attendees about whether or not we have the power to forgive sins.

I wanted to leave and walk directly into traffic.

These conferences only happen occasionally, though, and the rest of my seven months at home give me time to finally dig into the wealth of video footage and photos captured during my last two trips. I'm able to cut and assemble a tribute video for the ministry that sent Beth and the other VIPs to India, and they are so moved they plan to send their own video team to get more footage of this work they are doing in partnership with my company. This, for me, feels like a grand slam. I couldn't be prouder.

It's not too long before I get a call from my CEO. He informs me that in six months the company will return to the conference we attended in Delhi last year, but this time the conference organizers have requested one of our marketing representatives to lead a workshop for attendees about using storytelling techniques in marketing strategies for churches, ministries, and nonprofits. And, as I am the only marketing team member with this knowledge and experience slated to attend, they've asked me if I would do the honors.

This won't be surprising for you to hear at this point, but I'm not a good public speaker. I'm not even a good *regular* speaker. I panic when I have to speak in front of more than three people. My body shakes and forgets to breathe, and it makes my voice warble like I'm about to cry. In reality, I'm not emotional; I'm just suffocating a little bit.

But I don't even have to think about whether the tigress would accept this assignment. I pounce on the opportunity, and even though we're months out, I immediately start preparing.

The first thing I decide to do is join a local club that will give me an opportunity to practice speaking in front of strangers weekly. The club is on the small side with usually no more than ten to twenty people present, which is perfect; that will likely be the size of the group that will attend my workshop at the conference. I'd rather not do this alone, so I plan to recruit a friend to attend the weekly meetings with me. How can I pitch this in a way that will convince anyone to come, though? Describing it sounds like I'm relating a nightmare: "Every week, I have to give a speech in front of a bunch of strangers in a room lit by fluorescents . . ."

Tim is not game. I pitch the public speaking club to a few others, but they're out too. The only person who is even remotely interested is Ashley, who's always game for anything, but she can't swing it with her schedule. Long story short, I bite the bullet and attend on my own for six months, right up until the week that I leave for India.

And here's the God's honest truth: it never gets easier. Week after week, I corner my anxiety like it's a wild stallion and wrestle it into some semblance of submission, just long enough to get through the meeting. My hands shake and my voice wavers and my mind blanks every time I stand at the front of that room, even as the other members evolve from strangers to friends. Even as they consistently coach and encourage and support me.

This very physical reaction to speaking in front of people is not going away or even easing up despite my regular practice. I start to realize I need to get used to this feeling of my panicked, anxiety-riddled heart thundering out of my chest, *and* I need to be able to speak and think rationally when it happens. If it's not going away, I have to find a way to become comfortable in the chaos.

So I join a cardio-centric gym. I settle on a place with a lot of structure: I have to commit to class times, I'm penalized if I don't show up, and I don't need to make any decisions when I get there. The coaching staff does all the accountability tracking and programming. Plus, they have these nifty armbands that send your heart rate to your treadmill monitor so you can watch your beats per minute (BPM) rise and fall.

Stepping on the treadmill for the first time, I see it doesn't take long for my heartbeat to quicken. I know this feeling so well, but this time it's not because of anxiety or other emotional distress. It's because of my pace—but physically it feels the same. The tightness of my chest, the eruption of my heart, the static that drowns my brain in shadows.

Watching the BPM on my monitor, I try to use my breathing to control and steady my heart, bringing the number down. I test different breathing patterns, watching my BPM either rise or fall. And I rehearse parts of my presentation in my mind.

All the times I joined a gym in the past were to make myself thinner, smaller. To diminish the amount of space I took up, shrink my presence. This is the first time I have walked into a gym with the intent to make myself *more*: to take up more space, to be better heard, to make my presence bigger. It feels so good.

And while the cardio portions of the workout help me learn how to manage the roar of my anxiety, the weight lifting portions become my favorite. That rack of dumbbells whispers, "Go heavy, tiger. You're capable of more than you think you are." So I do. And I discover I am.

After a few weeks of consistent workouts and torturous speech meetings, I start to feel like I've made a sliver of progress. Instead of cornering the stallion called anxiety, it feels more like I'm starting to understand it better. Instead of trying to wrestle it into nothingness, I'm learning how to adjust myself to its movements.

To find a kind of flow in the frantic storm.

This next trip to India (Tim is coming for a portion again) is scheduled across October 31, and I am sad that I am going to miss my favorite time in my favorite place: autumn at home. As a kid I was never allowed to participate in Halloween because it glorified darkness and fear, and I was told those things weren't becoming of evangelical Christians. Now that I am an adult, adrift in the tides of spiritual in-betweens, it's become my favorite holiday. On a practical level, it doesn't require us to travel long distances, fill up our calendars with events, or give gifts like all the other holidays. We like those holidays too, but compared to them autumn is a blank slate that Tim and I fill with our own traditions in our own little community.

We live in the foothills of the Appalachians, a place that explodes with color in the fall. After months of blistering Georgia summer, those first cool winds that slip through the trees feel downright paranormal.

They raise the hair on my skin and resurrect me every year. We throw open all our windows and let those winds rush through our house like the ghosts of rowdy kids, slamming doors and dancing in the curtains. Our walls ring with Fleet Foxes, Hozier, Alison Krauss & Union Station, and vintage Coldplay. We make the switch from iced lattes to mugs of hot coffee in the morning. The sound of bare feet on our wooden floors is dampened by thick socks.

This autumn, there's a small but significant shift in my soul. I mentioned near the start of this story how in the year or so after the Breaking I developed an overwhelming fear of death. When I first brought up this issue in my therapy sessions, I half expected my therapist to give me a soothing speech or a gentle, comforting exercise to neutralize the fear. That's not what happened at all.

She was, of course, comforting and gentle. But essentially, her spirit embraced mine, then turned me back to look once more into the face of that void—that inevitability that awaits us all. She held me there with her hands on my shoulders. And she introduced me to the Stoic mantra: *memento mori.* "Remember, you must die."

I think the difference in her approach with me, compared to how she might have handled another, may have been due to the fact that the fear of death is a wholly different kind of anxiety. It is not outgrown or reasoned away. It is not the same as being anxious or fearful about something that may never happen. This is being anxious about the only thing that is guaranteed to happen in a human life.

But, my therapist explained, unlike some other types of anxiety, this particular kind of fear is fuel. High-octane fuel that can be used to create a wild and beautiful life, if you have the strength to tap it, the courage to harness it. "Remembering that this all must end, how then will you spend your precious few days? Remembering that this could be over at any time, what will you do? Who will you become?"

This is what she taught me: stop fearing an inevitability you cannot control—fear instead the squandering of your moments in the sun.

Memento mori didn't immediately help alleviate my death anxiety. Not at all. It sat like a rock in my shoe for months. But this autumn, I fished it out and began to understand. The way of life it demands isn't so different from the way of the tigress.

But I'd been gritting my teeth and muscling through this "season of the tigress," subconsciously assuming it wouldn't last forever. As much as the idea of the tigress gave me an anchor or a focal point, I also thought that, like Pi, I'd eventually find a soft, warm beach to collapse upon. My tigress, no longer needed, would saunter off into the jungle like Richard Parker, and I'd live the rest of my life healed and brave and sure.

But *Life of Pi* is fiction and an imperfect allegory for my journey. Memento mori paradoxically reminds me that I'm playing a much longer game, if I'm lucky. I'm not going to be chasing the tigress for a season; I'll be on her heels until that last breath, whether that is tomorrow or in seventy years. This is it, and it's spectacular and agonizing and gorgeous and hard and confusing. It's me trying and failing and trying again. It's breath burning in my lungs. It's my heart roaring in my ears, its voice the same when I'm in a panic as when I'm in ecstasy. And all of that together means my time isn't over yet.

I get it all, the bliss and the pain, for one more glorious day.

In the Middle Ages, memento mori was woven into art as dancing skeletons or dancing reapers. They cavort with people from all social tiers, from all walks of life, with kings and with street kids. The original intent was to remind onlookers of the fragility and brevity of life, of the fact that death does not discriminate. It dances with everyone sooner or later.

Dancing skeletons are a visual motif we still see around Halloween today. And even if the original intent behind the visuals has been watered down, they strike a chord in me. They remind me, "Memento mori. You don't have long. Find out who you are, and make your days count."

Growing up, I was told that Halloween honored death. I don't think that's true of every trick-or-treating household, but as of this autumn, it's true of mine. I raise a glass to the void, whatever it is that waits for me. I thank him for the reminder that these days of mine are limited, and I ask him to be patient. I'll dance with him soon, but I've got some things to do first.

The final thing on my pre-trip to-do list: research and shop for the right outfit to wear during my workshop presentation. This isn't a girlie indulgence; buying clothes as a professional woman is difficult. You don't want something that says, "Look at me" so much as you want something that says, "Listen to me." And it turns out that basically doesn't exist anywhere. I settle on a dark floor-length dress with a leather jacket and matching belt. You can't help but feel badass and capable in a leather jacket.

Not long before the trip, however, I get some troubling news: the media team of our partner ministry (the one sent to get more footage after viewing my tribute video) was stopped upon their arrival in Delhi by Indian security. They were questioned and ultimately denied entry into the country. After spending those twenty-five hours traveling around the globe, they had to turn right around and get on another flight out of the country. It's unclear if they'll ever be able to get into India.

India is aggressively defensive of its image as it's portrayed to the rest of the world; this is why they've gone to great lengths to report that leprosy is eradicated within their borders. Maybe the media team packed a large amount of video equipment, and it spooked the agents. There's also a chance that the ministry's name was used on paperwork or stamped on luggage, and that flagged the team for entry, even potentially causing them to be blacklisted. At the time of this writing, India is reported to be one of the top ten most dangerous places in the world to proselytize Christianity. I most definitely did not know that when I took this job, and I wonder what I would have done had I known. My story could have been quite different.

Learning the media team's story awakens my anxiety, and I start to sweat just thinking about the next time I'll walk through Indian customs. When I go through security in Atlanta, pulling out all the individual pieces of camera gear I still insist on hauling around in my carry-on, the alarm bells in my brain start up right on cue. *This will be my fourth time doing this,* I try to remind them rationally. *I've never had a problem. It will be fine.*

I hope it will be fine.

17
Custard Apples

Bleary-eyed and exhausted, Tim and I disembark from our plane and walk into the Bengaluru airport at 2:11 AM local time. Even in the middle of the night, India is wide awake.

We weave through the bustling terminals to the customs checkpoint. The weight of all the camera gear bites into my shoulders and compresses my lower back as we stand in line, waiting for an agent to call us forward. Finally, one beckons halfheartedly, and I make my way to his desk. Not long after Tim is waved over to another agent. I hand my entry agent my passport and my visa, trying not to think about the media team who were denied entry. I attempt to keep my face at ease, comfortable, but I can feel my jaw clenching.

The agent takes a minute to type into his computer. I look over at Tim and can see him putting his passport back into his backpack and moving away from his entry agent's desk. A red notice box pops up on my agent's computer screen, and he turns to me. "What is the purpose of your trip, ma'am?" he brusquely asks me.

My heart's in my throat. None of the other agents have ever asked me this. Tim's already on the other side of the "no re-entry" barrier. "I'm visiting friends," I say before really thinking it through—forgetting that

I just gave the agent a business visa. But it's not a complete lie. I am in Bengaluru to visit Danesh and Anika. They are my friends.

"Who?" he asks, and I tell him.

"These friends you are visiting, what do they do?" he pushes.

"Anika stays at home with her kids, and her husband, Danesh, works in audio production, I think," I answer. Still all technically true.

"And what do you do?" he demands.

"I work in marketing," I answer, my mouth very dry, and decide to add, "I'm a photographer," in case he asks to look inside my bulging backpack. Better not to have any surprises if we get to that point.

But, thankfully, we don't. He turns back to his computer and types on his keyboard a bit more, then hands back my passport without a word, and the barriers open.

"Thank you," spills out of my mouth as I walk through, clutching my passport in my sweaty hand, trying not to walk too quickly. Tim's eyes are a little wider than normal as I come up to him.

"I could see his computer screen," he murmurs. "It went all red when he scanned your passport. I wonder what that's about."

"Hopefully it was just a random spot check, and I'm not flagged," I say, taking a deep breath. There is still one flight we need to catch in a few days from Bengaluru to Hyderabad, the location of the conference, and I'm not interested in getting stopped again when a second security checkpoint runs my visa through the system.

———

The next morning we wake up to see our phones loaded with notifications from our doorbell camera back home. As it's a slow day, we take our time lazily scrolling through the videos of hopeful trick-or-treaters. A lot of them have coats on. The chilly autumn wind there must have been strong for so many parents to die on the wear-a-jacket-over-your-costume hill.

After breakfast (with two cups of chai each), Tim and I make the walk around the block to Danesh's place. There's nothing on the schedule today. No video shoots. No meetings. We're just spending the day with our favorite family in Bengaluru. We end up watching a Bollywood movie with Danesh, Anika, and the kids, enjoying the snacks Anika lays out on the coffee table.

"Do you enjoy these kinds of movies, Anika?" I ask her. The movie we just watched, *Bahubali*, was a sweeping fantasy epic culminating in the clash of armies and the forging of heroes. She offers a halfhearted shrug-nod, so I add, "What kind of movies do you like to watch?"

"I really like horror," she says sweetly.

"Really?!" Tim laughs. Anika is so soft-spoken and gentle, you'd never expect that to be her favorite. But she nods, smiling, and we swap scary recommendations.

Later that night Anika makes *dosas* for everyone. They are a classic South Indian food, similar to crepes: large, thin, griddle-baked batter that is rolled up and served with chutneys and sauces. The batter is made from lentils soaked overnight, idli rice, and sometimes potato. You tear off a piece of the hot, buttery dosa and use it to dip and scoop up runny side dishes.

Tim is tearing through his second when I ask Anika if she'll teach me how to make them. She leads me back into the kitchen with a smile. With steady hands, she shows me how to spread the batter across the griddle with the bottom of the ladle before drizzling spoonfuls of melted ghee on top. She slides a metal spatula under the goldening batter and starts rolling it up into a loose tube. As it cools, it gradually settles on itself, looking more like a very thin omelet.

The hot dosas smell buttery, crispy, comforting. And although they only have the buttery griddle in common, they remind me of the grilled cheese sandwiches my mom used to make on her homemade bread.

"You can get newspaper dosas," Anika says, swirling another ladle of batter across the griddle, "from some street vendors with large griddles. They are called that because they are as big as a page out of a newspaper."

We deliver the fresh batch of dosas to the dining room table. The kids show us which chutneys and sauces are their favorites and how to get the perfect ratio of dosa to sauce. On our first trip to Bengaluru, Danesh had tried to teach us how to eat like a proper Indian: no utensils, just your fingers. The average Indian transports food from plate to mouth with their deft fingertips, even saucy or rice-dominated dishes like biryani. My anxiety had kept me from trying this Indian way of eating—up until now. Now I tear, dunk, dip, and scoop.

It's not that the anxiety is suddenly and completely gone. It's still there, buzzing just below the surface. But I'm gradually building up a habit of trust: in myself, in the people around me . . . and even in God (or the universe, or fate, or whatever name you'd give to a benevolent force that pulls everything toward itself).

And this new habit of trust has created momentum. At some point the culmination of all my rewarded risks and gambles became a current that is starting to outpace the riptide of my anxiety. We finish the evening chatting over soothing mugs of tea brewed with mint leaves and lime.

———————————

The next morning Danesh, Satvik, Tim, and I are driving through the rural landscape outside the city. "What's Up" by 4 Non Blondes blares through the car speakers. We are returning to one of the rural communities we visited during our previous trips and are taking turns selecting the songs to listen to along the way.

This was Danesh's pick. It's a bit of a surreal moment, watching the landscape of rural India whiz by while the four of us sing, Danesh and Satvik lending a special flair with their Indian accents:

And so I wake in the morning
And I step outside
And I take a deep breath, and I get real high

We pass two men, both in flip flops, on a motorcycle, a live black goat held between them. Its belly on the seat, legs sticking straight out on either side of the vehicle.

And I scream at the top of my lungs
What's going on?

The moment feels so random and impossible, like it's a dream.

On either side of the road lines of short, scrubby trees stretch out into the rocky landscape. Women and men dressed in brightly colored sweeps of fabric walk in and around the trees, baskets hoisted on their shoulders and heads. Inside the baskets are mounds of light green produce that look like pale artichokes.

"What are they carrying?" I ask Danesh. In answer, he slows the car and pulls off onto the shoulder, right next to one of the fields full of trees. A man runs up to him with a plastic grocery bag full of the green things. Danesh pays the man and says, "These are custard apples. Want to try one?"

Inside the bag is a pile of round fruits, each about the size of a grapefruit. They are made up of smaller rounded segments clustered tightly together, like a huge, light-green blackberry. Satvik and Danesh each grab a fruit and bisect it easily with their hands, the tearing making a soft squelch. The fruit inside is pale yellow and soft, but not super juicy. Once they're opened, I can see that each of the rounded segments contains a long black seed, about the size of an almond, embedded into the flesh of the fruit.

I've never even heard of custard apples before. Tim takes one look at the seeds and decides he can't do it. Their shiny exterior and the way they are clustered together does have a certain hive-like quality that is hard to ignore. But I decide to give it a try.

Satvik and Danesh show me how to scoop a handful of the segments into my mouth, savor the flesh of the fruit, then spit out the seeds. I mimic them. The custard apple tastes mild and sweet, similar to a banana. The soft flesh is still warm from being in the sun, and the seeds are slippery on my tongue. I spit them out and enjoy a few more mouthfuls, mostly for the novelty of tasting a fruit completely foreign to my tastebuds. A fruit that was growing for weeks before I got here, fed by Indian rain and sunshine, and ripe just in time to arrive at Danesh's driver-side window.

It feels good to remember that there are things on this planet, my home planet, that I still haven't gotten to experience. Haven't seen yet, haven't tasted yet, haven't even heard their names yet. But they could be getting ready right now. Just waiting for me to arrive and savor them.

After several hours of driving, we arrive at the first community we visited on our last trip, the one that set off fireworks to welcome our van of board members. Our goal this time is to speak with people, Satvik acting as our translator, see how the audio Bibles they received are impacting them, and capture their stories on camera if they'd like to share. We also brought supplies for another huge biryani feast.

Many people are eager to tell their stories. They talk about their diagnosis, the impact of being ostracized, and what their faith has meant to them on their journey. Incredible, all too valid stories. Stories that the Indian government would maybe rather not surface. So many people volunteer to share them with us that we burn through all our batteries before we've heard from everyone.

This rattles me, and my anxiety surges loudly for a moment. I don't want anyone to feel like their story is not important or worth documenting. But we improvise and capture the last few interviewees by rigging up our iPhones until they, too, run out of battery.

As the sun starts to sink low in the sky, we pack up all our gear, bobble our heads in thanks to our gracious hosts, and pile back into Danesh's car to head back to the city. Tim and Satvik fall asleep in the backseat almost immediately.

Danesh turns to me. "Tomorrow night," he says, "we are going to a wedding." A cousin or family friend is getting married, and Danesh, Anika, and the kids have planned to go. "Would you and Tim like to come with us?"

I don't even have to think. "Yes, we'd love to attend an Indian wedding with you!"

On our last night in Varanasi during our first trip (the same night I started experiencing gastrointestinal illness), there was a wedding in one of the ballrooms of our hotel. It had been mid-April, the beginning of a popular wedding season for Hindus, Adnan explained at the time. The sounds of drums and fireworks and revelry reverberated through the night and into the early hours of the morning.

The wedding we are to attend with Danesh and his family, though, is a Christian wedding; while we shouldn't expect some of the Hindu customs, I'm excited to see the flair that Indian culture imbues into the event. Even the fact that Tim and I have been extended an invite through another guest is a huge shift—that would never happen in the States.

I put on the outfit I bought to wear to teach my workshop. Tim is able to get a more formal getup at a nearby mall in Bengaluru. Walking into the banquet hall, we're the only Westerners, and I can feel eyes drawn to us. Everything is elaborately decorated: draping curtains and strings of tiny lights everywhere. The carpet is red and gold, the quintessential Indian color scheme. The ceremony is highly formal, mainly Christian in this case, yet with serious rituals and speakers in a native Indian language. I occasionally glance at Danesh and Anika and try to pick up context clues from their expressions. The bride is beautiful, dressed in a modest Western white dress instead of the Hindu norm of a red and gold sari. At the end of the ceremony, the bride and groom exchange rings but don't kiss. That's a little too risqué for this more conservative community, Danesh later explains.

"What were all the different speakers saying during the course of the ceremony?" I ask him afterward while we're waiting our turn to approach the extravagant buffet.

He shrugs. "I don't know."

"Wait, they weren't speaking a language you know?"

"No, I only speak Tamil and Hindi," he clarifies.

And English, I think. That's so impressive. I can only speak English and a smidge of useless Latin. During our road trip the day before, "Despacito" by Justin Bieber came on, and Danesh asked us what the word meant. He thought we might know some Spanish since we live so close to Mexico, but we didn't have a clue. I had to look it up.

Danesh, Anika, and their exceedingly well-behaved kids were sitting through the whole wedding just as clueless as Tim and me. It's a reminder of just how vast the language barrier is in India, with her thousands of languages and dialects. It's hard to imagine driving one hundred miles from my home to Chattanooga, Tennessee, and not being able to speak the same language as anyone upon my arrival. And yet, that's how it is in many parts of India.

"Hey, Tim Tim." Danesh's face takes on the same quality it had when he tried to trick me into drinking hand-washing water. I don't remember when he started saying Tim's name two times in a row when addressing my husband. The trip before this one, maybe? We like it though. "What do you call someone who can speak three languages?"

"Trilingual," I answer before Tim, because I'm a know-it-all with no self-control. Danesh's eyes sparkle in my direction.

"What about someone who can speak two languages?" he continues.

"Bilingual," Tim answers this time.

"And what about someone who can only speak one language?"

We're quiet for a minute, digging around in our brains for the right term when Danesh lands the punchline: "An American." He tries not to grin too big as we roll our eyes and smirk.

All of us wind our way out of the banquet hall into the adjacent corridor, where the buffet lines have died down. A young boy, no more than twelve years old, latches onto Tim and follows him for the rest of the night. He can't speak much English, but Tim is patient. He takes selfies at the request of his little friend, following the boy's mimed instructions to cross his arms in front of his chest and give the camera a very serious look.

"Danesh, what's *gajar halwa?*" I ask, eyeing a warming tray of steaming, bright orange mush sprinkled with slivered almonds.

"Gajar is carrots," he explains, "and halwa is like a sweet dessert." So a sweet carrot dessert. I decide to try a modest serving of the concoction.

"This is how you must do it." Danesh steps beside me with a conspiratorial grin, scoops up a dollop of vanilla bean ice cream sitting in a bin of ice at the end of the buffet, and drops it on top of the steaming orange substance on my plate.

"Mmm, *à la mode*," I say with raised eyebrows. See, I know language stuff too.

Danesh has steered me right. The flavor of the gajar halwa is similar to carrot cake: sweet, earthy, warm with spices like ginger and cardamom. The coolness of the ice cream cuts through the heat of the silky halwa, its sweetness balancing out the spices. It reminds me of pumpkin, sweet potato, butternut squash...all those flavors of my favorite season, but still different enough.

It's the taste of autumn in India.

The day has come to leave Bengaluru behind and head to Hyderabad for the conference. Every sleep has brought me one step closer to the conference, my workshop, and the inevitability of my chest tightening, my heart racing as I stand to speak in front of people.

Danesh and his newest employee, Jai, will attend the conference as well. Jai is young, younger than Tim and I, so maybe early twenties. A bright kid, he zips around Bengaluru on his beloved black motorbike and strums worship songs on his guitar in his free time. His dark hair sweeps over the tops of his trendy thick-rimmed glasses. It will be good to see people we know in a new city, but Tim and I are leaving Bengaluru a day before them so I can be available to my Indian colleagues as they set up their booth in the conference's vendor hall.

We arrive at the impossibly busy Bengaluru airport only to learn that IndieGo, one of the main airlines here, has had a massive computer failure causing delays from passenger check-in all the way to the flight tower. The lines stretch all the way outside the building and onto the sidewalk where taxis and tuk-tuks drop off passengers. My anxiety rears its head, and I do my best to steady my breathing as we slowly wade through the crush of bodies and finally make it to check-in. Thankfully, no more computer screens turn red when my passport is scanned.

We hit the bathroom before jumping into the long security lines. All the stalls feature squatty potties, but I don't even think twice before using them. My legs are so much more trustworthy now thanks to the gym, and after encountering squatty potties so many times on these trips back and forth to India, my aim is pretty good too. No silicone funnel necessary.

The typical airport security in India is not like American airport security. In the same way that men and women have separate trains in Delhi, men and women have separate security lines here. Female security officers attend to the female line, and male security officers attend to the male line. Tim and I part to join our separate security lines. He always gets through security before I do, and today is no different. For whatever reason, the women's line is always significantly longer than the men's.

I wait for my turn to walk through a metal detector and into a small, curtained-off area no more than ten or twelve square feet where a female security officer dressed in army fatigues stands ready to pat me down. I hardly notice the eyes drawn to my Western jeans. I've grown accustomed to India's stares. A woman a few spots ahead of me in line stares blatantly over her shoulder into my face, and I smile back, meeting her eyes until she smiles and turns away.

I'm fairly certain that when the detector goes off after I walk through, it's been tripped by the metal zipper on the front of my bra. Rather than experience a rather intimate pat down in an isolated area, I show the female security officer the offending fastener.

She pats me down anyway. Geez, maybe I'm not totally accustomed to India yet. There's always something new for me to experience, something to push me outside my cozy little comfort zone. Something to keep me growing.

"All good?" Tim asks when I reach him on the other side of the checkpoint.

"I think I just got to second base with the security officer."

"Nice." He laughs, and we head to our gate.

18
I'm Okay

We land in Hyderabad right before dusk and take in the same busyness, the same urban sprawl that we experienced in so many other Indian cities. Our Uber driver speeds up onto an elevated highway that gives us a view of Hyderabad's rooftops. Suddenly, in the distance, a spray of dark shapes explodes up onto the horizon from the buildings below, swirling and shifting like smoke.

"Oh my God, are those bats?"

They are. Hundreds and hundreds of them, and they are huge. Even from far away I can make out their peaked, angular wingspans—exactly the way Count Dracula would have shaped his.

I would later look up "bats native to India," and I think what we saw was a colony of Indian Flying Foxes. The name is well-earned: they truly look like a fox ditched its bushy tail and traded its front paws for sinuous, clawed wings. At sixteen inches tall, they are some of the largest bats in the world. Their wingspans can reach almost five feet across. Rust-colored fur covers their bodies, and their faces are dominated by big, dark, round eyes.

I think they are adorable. Just a few months after our visit, however, a Hyderabad publication would run an article about the nuisance and danger that these animals sometimes pose to city residents. But in the moment I first see them, I can't help but feel a sense of awe and mystery.

Our hotel is connected to the conference center, and when we arrive, it's buzzing with activity. The coordinators look haggard and serious as they direct people to set up chairs, booths, banners, and tech equipment. Looking around, I'm not sure how the space is going to be ready in time for the thousand-something attendees tomorrow. It's the night before, and all I see is a huge ballroom with a stage being assembled on one side and, just outside the ballroom, an empty exhibit hall. But that's not for me to worry about, thankfully.

Tim retreats to our hotel room while I help my team set up our booth in the exhibit hall. Before leaving for dinner, I touch base with the coordinators about where I should be tomorrow for my workshop. I'd sent emails trying to get this information weeks ago as I prepared my presentation, but I wasn't ever able to get any hard answers.

It's no different now. The person I manage to corner doesn't know where I'll be or if I'll have the equipment needed to show my presentation, and they're too overwhelmed with their workload to help me track down the answers. "Just be down here at the tech booth in the ballroom early tomorrow before the conference starts, and someone should be able to help you." That's all they can tell me while walking away to put out another more pressing fire.

I can feel my chest start to tighten and my heart race as I head out of the hall toward the hotel to grab dinner with Tim in the adjoining restaurant. He tells me he booked us a massage at the onsite spa for later that night, even before he learned how stressed the conversation with the coordinator has made me.

"I figured you would need to relax." He smiles. My kind, intuitive partner.

Afterward, I pour over my presentation notes until I fall asleep.

Morning comes quickly. I wake up before my alarm; anxiety has found me everywhere—unconscious, subconscious, and conscious. As I get ready, I worry my bottom lip until it bleeds. I'm anxious about being late, about what I don't know, about what I might forget, about not being able to use my presentation, about being asked questions I can't answer. About being viewed as a fraud.

But I've worked hard. I've gained a lot of knowledge that I now get to share, I remind myself. That's enough.

I deserve to be here.

I deserve to be here.

I deserve to be here.

Curling my hair and applying my makeup, I try to compartmentalize. This is a Christian conference, and I know some of my anxiety is coming from the fact that I feel like an outsider in that community. However, my workshop is about marketing and using narrative tools to support a compelling brand. It's a subject far removed from any type of faith-related topic, so I do my best to set aside that particular concern for now.

My mind fails to rationally compartmentalize and dismiss the host of other worries buzzing in my brain, so I turn to my breath and imagine I'm watching the BPMs on my treadmill monitor drop as my heart settles into a more even, calm rhythm. By the time Tim and I head down to the conference hall, my hands are steady, at least.

Even though we're early, we have to navigate through a small crowd of attendees to get to the tech booth. We run into Danesh and Jai and a handful of my colleagues, who are all encouragement. I'm so grateful for this safe little tribe cheering me on.

When I get to the tech booth at the back of the huge ballroom—it somehow feels larger now that it has over a thousand seats lined up in front of the fully assembled stage—a frazzled woman with a clipboard walks up like she's been expecting me. She starts peppering me with questions about my presentation and what kind of equipment I'll need to run it.

When I ask her where the workshop will take place, she hesitates, her eyebrows scrunching closer together. "Here," she says. "On the main stage."

My insides melt, ice in the face of a blowtorch. My left ear pops as my blood pressure spikes. I focus on keeping my breath steady. All these sensations aren't strangers to me by now. "Oh," is all I can think to say. *This can't be correct.* "I thought I was leading a small workshop."

"Lauren, right?" She checks her clipboard, verifies my company's name. "Yes, you're our second keynote speaker this morning."

Keynote speaker?

"Oh . . ." I smile, and I hope it looks easy, effortless. A tiger's smile. "That's no problem. I can adapt what I prepared."

She nods, smiles back, doesn't seem worried. Not about me, at least.

As I walk away to sit with Tim near the stairs leading to the stage, my anxiety creates a storm of frantic static that tears through my head, making it hard to concentrate. I pull out my notes and try to think through the changes needed to transform my work into a keynote presentation. I had several planned moments where I had hoped to collaborate on an exercise with my workshop attendees. That would have to go. There were also moments when I'd hoped to inter-act with the attendees. Can I still keep that if I'm speaking to over a thousand people?

Over a thousand people. My brain stutters, my eyes drift away from my notes. My heart flutters like a bird trying to escape my ribs. I try to pull myself back from the brink of panic, to focus on adapting to this change I must face, but my body is telling me it just needs to sit with this new reality for a minute.

So I let it.

That minute stretches on for a small eternity. As the thou-sand-somethings start filtering in and finding their seats. As the lights start to dim. As the first keynote speaker finishes and walks down the steps of the stage to thunderous applause.

I feel my feet walk up those same steps, my shoulders pull back, and my face turn to meet the spotlight.

A half hour later I descend those steps to my own round of applause. And I immediately want to run. Away. Away from here. *Home.*

But I smile and force myself to walk smoothly back to my seat. I can see Danesh and Jai. They're clapping, smiling at me, and the emcees' voices behind me are ushering the audience onward toward the next part of the conference.

It's done. I'm done. I don't remember a lot of my presentation; my brain locked me out and took over the whole time I was on stage. My voice shook, I do remember that—the pseudo-emotional warble I never could out-practice, never could outrun at the gym. I remember trying to dip into casual, unscripted elaboration during one of my points and getting lost in my own ramblings. And I ran over one of my slides too quickly for anyone to get anything out of it.

But I did it. Tim beams and tells me I did great.

For the rest of the day I feel outside myself. I anchor myself near Tim, Danesh, and Jai even as conference attendees approach me to shake my hand, take a selfie, and ask me elaborating questions about my presentation. Everyone is kind and enthusiastic. I match their energy, and I'm so grateful to connect with them. But I'm also exhausted. Drowning in a bravery hangover. Where did that bravery even come from?

As the day starts to draw to a close, the vendor and conference halls shut down, and attendees, speakers, and exhibitors congregate in the hotel lobby and restaurant. Not really wanting to spend the rest of the night in my room but also looking for a little distance from the crowd, I'm flooded with relief when Danesh asks us if we want to leave. Go explore the city a bit and get dinner out.

We quickly change before meeting up in the lobby. I trade my business formal dress for a pair of loose overalls, pull my hair into a ponytail, and grab my camera, slipping back into my more comfortable tourist persona like it's a pair of worn house shoes. I'm able to sneak through the hotel lobby without anyone stopping me to talk, and the four of us take an Uber to a local landmark in the Islamic part of the city, the Charminar.

Charminar means "four minarets," and that's essentially what it is: four minarets almost two hundred feet tall, joined together to support a second story. Huge archways sweep up to a point between the domed towers. Built in 1591, the second story was used as a mosque for over four hundred years, but eventually the religious gatherings were relocated, and the Charminar became a Hyderabad landmark and tourist attraction.

We wade through a crush of people toward the scaffolded old-world architecture. It looks like some repairs are being made, but nevertheless, it's an incredible monument. Underneath the arches men peddle scarves, water, toy dogs that squeak loudly, and platters of samosas held aloft on their heads.

Tim and I are the only Western tourists I see. Based on their clothes and the languages they're speaking, most of the sightseers seem to be from this continent, many of them wearing traditional Islamic garments. Women in floor-length black *abayas* with *shaylas* or *hijabs* covering their heads glide around the courtyard, holding tight to children's hands.

We venture up one of the narrow spiral staircases that wind inside the minarets leading up to the monument's second story. Looking out over the city, we can just make out the sun, a broad mandarin orb sliding toward Hyderabad's rooftops. The smog is so thick I can stare directly into the sunset without hurting my eyes.

As I gaze from the height of the Charminar at the crowd thrumming below me, I'm suddenly struck. An overwhelming adoration for this country and her people, stronger than I've ever felt before, seizes my heart and locks up my throat. This place that's seen so many versions of me and lovingly held each one, her hands abrasive but, at the same time, healing. Terrifying, but tender.

A young girl with a sparkly yellow hijab, dark eyes, and freckles on her nose interrupts my thoughts. She shyly asks to take a selfie with me, and I blink clear my glossy eyes for the photo.

My little group and I enter another narrow staircase that leads back down to the street, but about halfway we come to a dead stop on the stone steps. The doorway at the bottom is blocked. The minaret is so narrow I can touch both walls without extending my arms. We're all standing in single file, Tim towering in front of me even though he's on a lower step. Another man towers behind me, standing so close I can feel his breath in my hair.

I remember when this would have caused me to panic not so long ago.

But I'm okay.

Curiously, impossibly, miraculously, inconceivably. The cool steadiness of my heart in this moment is so foreign, it fascinates me.

I'm okay.

The Islamic areas of Indian cities are the place to go if you're looking to eat meat. Hindus are vegetarian, so there are no slaughterhouses or butcher shops in their communities. Muslims, however, have no religiously mandated adherence to vegetarian principles. Since we're already in the Islamic quarter tonight, we head out in search of a dinner that we hope will include some beef, chicken, or mutton.

Danesh takes us to a biryani shop not far from the Charminar. Tim is flying back to the States in a few hours, so we all order big: chapati, biryani with boiled eggs and chunks of juicy beef and chicken, curries with basmati rice, samosas, and *gulab jamun*—a dessert similar to donut holes soaked in a sweet syrup.

"You must try Irani chai," Danesh implores us. "Hyderabad is famous for it." So we all order a round and wait for Danesh to tell us what makes this chai so special. The way it's made, he explains, is different from your typical Indian chai. It has something to do with the ingredients they choose, the method they use to make it.

Honestly, he undersold it. When our server finally sets a cup in front of me, I take a sip, and I'm blown away. I thought there was no way India could improve upon her most quintessential beverage, but I was so wrong. It's as delicious as a normal chai, with deep spices that almost bite in the back of your throat, but much sweeter, creamier, almost frothy. I could drink this every day and never get tired of it.

Night deepens around us. India's fluorescents and neons and head-lights ignite. The four of us sit in our cozy booth, Irani chais in hand, for as long as we can before we must relinquish the moment, load into a rickshaw, and return to the hotel.

I didn't know it at the time, but this would be my last trip to India for many years. At the very moment that I stood atop the Charminar, people living in China's Hubei Province were contracting an intense respiratory disease. That disease, eventually named COVID-19, would go on to lock down the entire planet in a pandemic the scope of which had not been seen in perhaps a hundred years.

Even though I had no idea what was coming, I still felt a profound sense of closure during this trip. I limped into this part of the world nearly two years ago afraid to be away from home, to get sick, to get sun-burned, to meet a stranger's eyes, to be seen. To confront the anger and doubt that followed me like a shadow. I was so afraid of everything.

And I finished this trip standing tall on a stage. By then I had known and survived sickness. My freckles had deepened in the sun. I had looked into the eyes of strangers, had almost always found grace there, and I let myself be seen by them. It wasn't that I stopped being afraid; I was still very often afraid. But somewhere along the way, my fear stopped calling the shots so much. I found something inside myself that could hold its own.

I learned to move in Anxiety's flow, not getting swept up by her undercurrent but cutting my own path away from victimhood and toward ownership. I walked into the hurricane of my own rage, my grief, my doubt, my mortality, and my assumptions about God, and I did not turn my face away.

It didn't stop the storm. I don't think this storm inside me will ever stop. But I did learn how to bend in the gales instead of letting them break me.

I also found the courage to walk deeper into the world of ministry despite my spiritual doubts and tumultuous professional history. And while I'm proud of the work I've done to give people access to the Red Letters, on this final trip, I started to feel that my days in the world of professional ministry were winding down.

Despite it all, I realized I had become the kind of woman who would have inspired and intimidated me just two years ago. The kind of woman that, for so long, I had believed was out of my reach.

The process almost never looked heroic. It often looked pitiful, like shaky hands and the ragged breaths of a panic attack. Like a defeated face reflected in a dirty train window. Like muffin crumbs and anger and split lips. Many times I failed to keep up with the tigress. But just like my body, my spirit and my mind got stronger, and I learned from every knockdown.

Now I have a practice I will delight in repeating wherever I am for as long as I live: try, fail, learn, and try again. And even if it no longer takes place on Indian soil, my own becoming will always feel like India—the place where a tigress taught me to trust.

Afterword

"There are years that ask questions, and there are years that answer."

—Zora Neale Hurston

Every year on the anniversary of the Breaking, the air in my house feels a little thinner than usual. Time, a little more translucent. I sit in the spaces in my home where, years ago, a shattered young woman wept for the loss of a future she'd hoped to have. Where the fabric of her spirit was rent, where her faith crumbled to ash in her hands. Where she got only silence in response.

It still hurts. Even with healing, the memory of the Breaking will still throb and ache and remind me of the broken woman I thought I'd always be.

I can almost hear her; she's still there somewhere inside of me. She'll always be there. But I wish I could reach through time, take her face in my hands, and tell her how this story was going to end. This is what I would tell her:

You're in a deep pit, but you will not be here forever. It's hard in this moment to believe it, but you *will* rise up off that floor. You'll do the hard, painful work to cauterize that wound threatening to bleed you out. And yes, it will burn like hell, and you will scream. Scream, baby—through gritted teeth and anger and anguish. Scream until your throat is raw with the injustice of it. When the smoke clears and your lungs finally give out, you'll wipe your eyes, you'll stand up, and you'll live.

It won't all be fixed after that. Not by a long shot. This will take time. You'll have to relearn how to trust other people and, more importantly, yourself. And this is an arduous, painful, time-consuming process, so be patient with yourself.

You'll stumble often, you'll know the taste of dirt, but you'll always rise. And with every rise, you'll get stronger. You wouldn't believe me if I told you how alike you are to all the heroines you've ever loved.

And I know it's a mean thing, a calloused thing, to say these words to you right now. I know you don't want to hear them. All you want is yesterday, that moment before the Breaking. You never asked to walk this path, even if it eventually ends in sunshine. That's okay. Take your time. Don't rush this. It may be mean to say this while you're still bleeding, but that doesn't make it a lie.

Something magical will happen to you in the years after this crushing blow. It will bloom through your overwhelming pain, your surging panic, your crushing despair. In time you will see that while you were pressed to the ground, white-knuckled, barely breathing—you became the person you were always meant to be.

The person you're becoming is brave. She has a voice, and she uses it. She feels at home in places she'd never expect. She rubs shoulders and locks eyes and holds hands with people so good and loving and true, they'll help her to trust again.

They'll help her to believe in the divine again.

I journaled and photographed my way through India completely unaware of the direction my story was headed. It was only years later when I went back through my writings that I started to see this story. I could see its pattern and the parts of it that made sense.

But the reality is we don't live storylines that wrap up neatly, with clear before and after pictures. I experienced tremendous healing and growth during these India years, but there are still moments now when I crumble, when I fail to show up, when I revisit rock bottom.

And that's okay. We're all in good company on this, and rock bottom is a solid, trustworthy surface off which to push when we're ready to try again.

There are days when I am all tiger stripes, fearless and ready. And there are many more days, still, when my anxiety is just too loud, my depression just too strong.

And God is there, in every one of them.

There are days when I believe, and my house rings with worship and prayer and wonder. And there are days when the void convinces me it gets the last word.

And God is there, in every one of them.

My favorite quote from *Life of Pi* may be my most favorite quote ever: "If you take two steps toward God, God runs to you." I have found this to be the truest thing. It may not look like you think it will; it almost certainly won't look the way a pastor on a stage tells you it will. Those two steps? They might be shuffling, hesitant, fearful, and small. Mine were.

But God won't look like a bearded man with rules and shame, a book he tells you to buy, and a small group you have to join. God running to you might look like two women in a boat on the Ganges desperately searching for your eyes. Seeking you out.

Or it might look like steady, unexpected hands unwinding all the messy, limiting, ill-fitting beliefs you've forced yourself to wear for so long, then redressing you with grace and liberation, pinning you with love, and asking nothing in return.

It might look like kids pulling you into their games and unexpected puppies with floppy ears and tails.

It might look like your friend razzing you about speaking only one language. It might look like your dog running to you with absolute joy and abandon when you finally get home from a trip.

Be ready before you take those two steps. Be ready to be surprised by the ways God runs to you.

We don't have to have all this figured out. Remember that. Even as we take those two steps, even as God runs to us. At no point are we expected to have all the answers. Just like with true, deep healing, all that is required of us is that we keep showing up.

True healing is glacially slow. It's an unhurried gradient, like a sunset. The dark and the light blend together, and at times it's hard to tell if you're still at the beginning of the struggle or if you're finally nearing the end.

But the cool relief of the evening will come. And just like day-veiled constellations, you'll notice beautiful things—and fierce tigers—inside of you that were there all along. You just couldn't see them.

Maybe that's how it is with God too.

Acknowledgments

I might be the only person I know who actually reads acknowledgments. Usually it's a chance to experience the author in a more intimate way, but if you've made it this far, we're already best friends. So, instead, let me introduce you to some people who made it possible for me to put this book into your hands.

David, Emily, and the Lake Drive team: David was so knowledgeable and patient with me as I inundated him with a hundred nervous questions about publishing this book. He took a chance on a no-name, wannabe writer with 666 Instagram followers, and now this book exists. I can't thank you enough, David.

Amanda and Stephanie, my editors: Amanda was the first to read this work as a rough, underdeveloped pile of thoughts. Her direction and encouragement were critical to getting me past that first major hump. And Stephanie, who got to play with a much more polished edition, helped me zero in on the heart of it all. You're both brilliant and lovely and wildly capable, thank you for your help.

My beta readers: that handful of people who rewarded my trust with their honesty and helped this be the best it could be—Sarah L., Rebecca, Kate, Sarah W., and Lydia. Sending someone a massive document and requesting they read it thoughtfully is a huge ask. Thank you, beautiful hearts. I appreciate each of you.

Danesh, Anika, and your entire family: you were dosas from heaven at a time when my soul was desperately starved. Thank you for feeding me.

Finally, my tribe: first, my best friends in the world, Joe and Ashley. You know it all, and you never left. Melissa, my therapist, who taught me to fight for me. My big, crazy bunch of in-laws who love me no matter what. Jonathan and Denise, my parents, who are always in my corner, even when I write hard stuff. My brothers, Chad, Ethan, and Josh, who will always be my favorites. And my sister, Bethany. My first and longest running soulmate. You make me brave.

And finally, Tim. This story isn't just mine. It is very much ours. Thank you for encouraging me to write it and then being brave when I decided I wanted to share it. Thank you for being so engaged, so devoted, and so supportive of me and this dream. I wouldn't have been able to do it without you, but I also wouldn't have wanted to. You're the best one. I got the best one.

About the Author

Lauren Cibene (laurencibene.com) is a doubtful-yet-hopeful Jesus person, gym rat, bookworm, and writer. She used to be a confident evangelical, a homeschool student, a foster mom, a world traveler, a professional photographer. Now she's a business co-owner and daylights as a conversion copywriter, penning words even non-readers read—descriptions on product packaging and Amazon pages—but she moonlights over on Substack. She lives with her husband near Atlanta.

About Lake Drive Books

Lake Drive Books is an independent publishing company offering books that help you heal, grow, and discover. We champion books about values and strategies, not ideologies, and authors who are spiritually rich, contextually intelligent, and focused on human flourishing. We want to help readers feel seen.

If you like this or any of our other books at lakedrivebooks.com, we could use your help: please follow our authors on social media, subscribe to their newsletters, and tell others what you think of their remarkable books.

www.ingramcontent.com/pod-product-compliance
Lightning Source LLC
Chambersburg PA
CBHW020240130626
46549CB00005B/1979